# BUCK
## AND
## THE
# Band
## OF
# Angels

And Other Funny, Moving, Inspiring
Stories from a Pastor's Life

## RUSSELL T. MONTFORT

*Abingdon Press / Nashville*

BUCK AND THE BAND OF ANGELS
AND OTHER FUNNY, MOVING, INSPIRING STORIES
FROM A PASTOR'S LIFE

**Library of Congress Cataloging-in-Publication Data**

Montfort, Russell T., 1928-
  Buck and the band of angels : and other funny, moving, inspiring
stories from a pastor's life / Russell T. Montfort.
    p. cm.
  ISBN 978-0-687-64517-6 (pbk. : alk. paper)
  1. Pastoral theology.   I. Title.
  BV4014.M58 2007
  253—dc22

                                                    2007009023

07 08 09 10 11 12 13 14 15 16—10 9 8 7 6 5 4 3 2 1
MANUFACTURED IN THE UNITED STATES OF AMERICA

# Contents

# Introduction

ACCESSING GOD IS NOT THE EASY THING THAT some say it is. Not for me, it isn't.

The Holy God of All That Is probably shouldn't be easily accessed. At least not in that total sense in which some say they experience God. They *know* God. They walk and talk and get up-to-the-minute memos from God—about available parking places, where their lost reading glasses are, and whether or not they should abscond with hotel linens—sheets, towels, and pillowcases.

My wife, Ruth, and I were traveling with a group in Italy; and one morning at breakfast a woman in our party made much ado about the pure linen sheets that belonged to the hotel where she, her husband, and the rest of our group were staying. She liked the sheets and pillowcases so much, she was considering taking them when she left for home. Several members of our group said we thought that was a bad idea, that it amounted to theft, and that it was illegal in Italy, just as it is illegal in the United States.

The next morning on the way to catch the plane back to the U.S., someone asked the woman if she had taken the sheets as planned. She laughed aloud and clapped her hands and said, "I completely forgot it until this moment. God just took that out of my head. God made me forget that."

God tells such people where to vacation, whom to marry, and whether they should move to Sioux City. I have this growing conviction that God has set me loose in this world to make those kinds of decisions myself. God has shaped the world, made it dependably wonderful, and taught me how to live in it while being morally responsible.

And God has been teaching me that life is good that way, never finished and never nailed down, eminently exciting and surprising. I think that much of the time we try to factor out the surprise in our lives. We don't want God to show us something new or strangely different because then we may have to reassess truth and redirect our energies.

It seems clear that the know-it-all-about-God crowd is actually a faithless crowd. They don't trust God. They say they do, but they don't. They have all these incantations, often characterized by what I call the "I jus' wanna" prayers: "Lord, I jus' wanna thank you...."; "Lord, I jus' wanna praise you..."; "Lord, I jus' wanna ask you...."; and then they outline the conditions of their belief. They believe that they can make God do anything they want God to do.

Once I heard an otherwise lovely spirited woman tell how she didn't want her first grader assigned to a certain teacher at their school, a dour, grumbly woman. The mother prayed mightily that it wouldn't happen, and it didn't. It never seemed to occur to her that her prayer had dumped some-body else's child into the witch's cauldron.

To say "God, I love you, I adore you, I worship you, I thank you" *and no more* is to trust that the God worthy of your love, adoration, worship, and thanks wishes you well, and with you as partner, will work out the details of your life. God will give you insight and strength, affection and courage, and will teach you patience. But the decisions are yours, acted out of a moral imagination rather then a set of rules.

At the end, you can lie down in peace, knowing that the same God also goes with you into the last great adventure, death. You won't have to go scrambling and begging for more chances, because you will know that God has honored the life you have lived and in advance has forgiven you where you blew it. Life and death are great adventures, not scripts.

In this book, we shall further explore that premise: life as an adventure, not a script. And how throughout this adven-ture God speaks to us in the stories of others—not just of bona fide saints, but of marginalized people as well. If you will allow yourself to be sensitized by the power of the liv-ing Christ, you may discover that he keeps on showing up in surprising people—numinously, and sometimes under astonishing circumstances.

# The Call

GOD SHOULD BE MORE SPECIFIC WHEN HE calls. Or when she calls. Whatever. The point is that God should be more specific. I ended up in the ministry as a result of a number of experiences that, when strung together, culminated in my becoming a preacher/pastor. But while the call itself was fairly clear, the details of how it would be lived out were not.

For instance, I didn't know about mimeograph machines (contraptions enjoying wide use in the days before copy machines and computer printers) or that you *had* to know how to operate one because every Sunday you needed a printed program. Even though the parishioners didn't particularly want it. After the initial service in one of my first churches, a pleasant old man went around and took up all the worship programs after church and brought them back to me with the report: "Preacher, I brung you your little papers back."

God should have been more specific about summer church camp too. I have trekked many miles on the Appalachian Trail with a forty-pound pack on my back, leading a pregnant donkey burdened with potatoes and tents and frying pans on her back while trailing a gladsome pack of teenagers. The farmer who owned the donkey said to me, after we had loaded her into a truck for the trip, "Now, preacher, that donkey is pregnant, and I don't remember whether she's due in a month, or a month overdue."

I have also slept on the ground under an open sky, having surrendered my sleeping bag to as many as three six-year-olds whom I had accumulated during the night as the result of an assortment of dismaying experiences. And I once spent an entire week at Camp Nixon on the Atlantic Coast near Cherry Grove Beach, South Carolina.

God was not specific in the call, or I would never have ended up at Camp Nixon. I think that hell will be operating a mimeograph machine for the first ten thousand years and the rest of the time will be spent at Camp Nixon, where they will have cable TV access but only two shows programmed: endless reruns of the PTL Club and, on alternating days, PBS fund-raisers.

The campers at Camp Nixon came from perfectly nice church families in a few piedmont North Carolina towns, but the combination of sea air, sand, and macaroni every night for dinner overwhelmed them. That, and I also suspected that some of them were sniffing bug spray.

I had fifteen-year-old boys in my cabin, all suffering from raging pubescence. They called me "Mulligan" and my nineteen-year-old college sophomore colleague-counselor-in-residence "Stew." There were two of us and sixteen of them, a distinctly disadvantageous ratio. We lived in a cabin named Whispering Pines.

At almost every meal the camp director, while making her announcements, would have something tacky to say about Whispering Pines—things such as "Whispering Pines was restless during quiet hour" or "I don't think Whispering Pines is practicing good hygiene." And then instead of looking at us, she would gaze in the direction of a banner hanging from the ceiling which said "Jesus Saves!" with some further information added to the bottom with spray paint: "and Moses Invests." She had a hunch that some denizen of Whispering Pines had done that, and it was a good hunch.

Time prevents me from telling you about the alligator in the lake where my Whispering Pines wards sneaked off to during rest hour and went swimming while I pretended to be asleep, or how they burned their names into the ceiling of the cabin on the last night, using candles left over from a touching fireside commitment service. And good taste dictates that I not tell you what their skit was at the closing campfire.

And that was just one summer. It's a good thing that God doesn't fill in all the details at the issuance of the call. What God does is give the call and then promises to be with you no matter what.

The important thing that was going on at Camp Nixon was that a group of adults had taken a piece of their lives, precious days that could never be retrieved, and invested them in an unruly bunch of teenagers. They organized a trip to the beach, kept the campers from danger (well, for the most part), listened to them, allowed them laughter; they did so in the name of Jesus, the one whose name was on the banner and of whom it was said that he saves.

# Virtue Gone to Seed

I DID MY UNDERGRADUATE WORK IN A LITTLE church college in Kentucky; it was immediately after World War II, and colleges still thought they should control your life and make you better than you wanted to be. Our college required us to attend chapel twice a week, and that requirement was the source of a lot of complaining. It was hard to require that kind of commitment from students who had just logged three, four, even five years of military service and, during that time, had acquired about twenty years of maturity.

To be honest, I didn't mind it all that much, though up to that time in my life, I had not been much of a churchgoer. I thought some of the speakers were interesting, and among those who were not, some were pretty funny—maybe unintentionally, but still . . . .

And besides, it was during that time in my life that I learned all the verses to the hymn "Are Ye Able, Said the Master?" It must have been the favorite of somebody whose duty it was to select the hymns, and we sang it at least once a week.

In chapel, Trudy Nichols was the attendance monitor for my section of seats. As a matter of fact, she sat right next to me, and I often trembled at the obvious pleasure with which she wrote down the name of some absentee.

My friend Bill sat on the other side of Trudy, and sometimes we would lean across her to convey messages or talk behind her. Which she didn't like very much. Trudy was one of those people who are absolutely virtuous. She did everything right. Except now and then she appeared wearing remarkable falsies—not always, just sometimes.

In class she always knew the answers, and she graduated *magna cum laude*. Some days I would get to chapel before Trudy and sit in her seat, next to Bill, so we could talk more easily. Trudy always objected; but, knowing that it annoyed her, I wouldn't move.

One spring day, I received a note from the dean of the college, summoning me to his office. When I arrived, there sat Trudy. According to the dean's records, Trudy and I had missed chapel five times already that semester, and the dean wanted an explanation.

I was dumbfounded; I protested loudly that I had been there every time. True to form, Trudy had an explanation. I had arrived early five times and had sat in Trudy's seat, which meant that Trudy had to sit in mine. By Trudy's righteous judgment, that meant that we were both absent.

That is virtue gone to seed.

I looked at her. She was serious. I wanted to say, "Get a

life, Trudy!" But there was the dean. He told me to sit henceforth in my own seat, and dismissed us.

Later in my life, I ran across a quotation from Lord Acton. It made me think of Trudy. He said "Every institution finally perishes by an excess of its own basic principle."

I sometimes think of how it is possible to perish at the hands of one's virtues. And not even know it.

# The Smallest of the Puppies

A S A SMALL BOY, I WAS A "RULES KEEPER." I wanted the approval of the "grown-ups." When I became one (a "grownup"), I was less certain that they knew what was really going on. I thought they were often misled by their own self-interest.

Later, in the late 1940s, I worked for two summers as an illustrator for a newspaper. For one account I did all the artwork and the copy. It was a weekly advertisement disguised as a column written by a woman who ostensibly had discovered certain items at a number of specialty shops. The shops all paid to have items mentioned. The column was titled: "Let's Go Shopping with Cherry Chase." I was Cherry Chase.

For one week's assignment I was supposed to illustrate a pair of women's black patent-leather pumps with a matching handbag. I was also to write the copy. I headed the piece "Black as Sambo" and highlighted the shine on the shoes and bag. The piece went right across my boss's desk for approval and on to the pressroom.

When I arrived at work the next morning, I was summoned to the office of the advertising director, where I joined a meeting of the managing editor of the newspaper, the director, his boss, and a representative of the local chapter of the NAACP, who was in the company of his attorney. The mood of the meeting was tense. The one thing they all agreed upon was the fact that it was my fault. I was the "naïve kid," a term first contributed by my immediate boss and thereafter used anytime one of the participants spoke of me. It was this "naïve kid" who had written the racist copy that had caused the paper to pull the ad so it would not appear in that evening's paper, and it was this "naïve kid" who as a result might bring about a lawsuit. Therefore, "the kid" (a sometimes used alternative to "naïve kid") had done something so stupid it was going to cause the newspaper to lose income.

If you have ever been around a newborn litter of puppies, in particular a large litter, you have noticed that there is usually one who is smaller than the others. He is consistently pushed out of the buffet line and, in general, is treated in ungracious ways by his siblings. He is unwelcome, unwanted, and *persona non grata*. He is sometimes even treated that way by his own mama. That's the way I felt that morning in the "Black as Sambo" inquisition—like a runt puppy, admired by and championed by none.

I *was* the offender, of course. It was I who wrote the copy and drew the illustration. It never occurred to me that it was racist. At that time, in that place, I had not yet been sensitized to all of the insulting things that were said about African American people. I had a lot of stuff to unlearn. I was, in fact, a naïve kid who provided the perfect foil for the anger, embarrassment, and righteous indignation of a bunch of "grownups."

Unfortunately, that was not the last time I was roughed up by the grownups (big dogs). Wherever folks are organized into systems, whether in companies, the military, or the church, it is important that blame be fixed, and it often is the runt who gets tagged.

For the rest of my professional life, I was for the most part able to maintain an uneasy peace with the "grownups." I worked assiduously to do as I was told and discovered early on that if I could remain objective about the dilemma in which I found myself, there often were some very amusing things going on.

When I finished college, I was trying to raise money to go to a theological seminary in another state, but my efforts weren't producing many results. About that time, the pastor of a large congregation in the largest city near my home called me and wanted to discuss with me a position on his pastoral staff.

We met for lunch in a suburban cafeteria near his church, where we went through the cafeteria line and found a table. He immediately took charge of the conversation, and though we didn't talk much about me and my particular abilities, we did talk about him, his considerable abilities,and his successful career. We discussed his career trajectory that just might make him into a bishop, which would mean that he might not be there for me after a couple of years.

About then is when he realized that some earlier diner had spilled blackberry cobbler on the seat of his chair. He came undone at the prospect of having to walk out of there with this big purplish-red stain on his blue seersucker pants. It had a little whipped cream in there too, or maybe it was vanilla ice cream. Actually, it made an interesting design, with the blue and white stripes and this big purple chrysanthemum superimposed. It would have looked good made up into draperies for the sunroom.

As we departed, he wanted me to walk up close to him so that no one could see the back of him, which I did. Walking so closely meant that I had to get in step with him or I might walk up on his heels. I laughed. We looked like a couple of clowns.

I had hoped to impress him; I never got a chance. He said he would call, but he didn't—very likely because I laughed. Little dog is not supposed to laugh at expense of big dog.

The parents of a college friend made it possible for me to go to the university of my choice. And in a couple of years, big dog was not elected bishop.

# The Funeral

ONE OF MY FIRST APPOINTMENTS AS PASTOR was to a group of four small churches. In the neighborhood of one of those churches was also a congregation of Primitive Baptists. The Primitive Baptists had no building of their own and little congregational life. It was a belief of theirs that too much church attendance would make you "hard-hearted." They had no Sunday school because they believed that the education of young Christians belonged in the home.

In that particular congregation, there was no church membership. As a matter of fact, if you followed their persuasion, you were called a "leaner" rather than a member. There was no roll with your name on it; you simply "leaned" their way.

From time to time, there would be a death in one of the families of that group somehow related to one of the families in our congregation, and a request would be made to hold the funeral in our sanctuary and the burial in our cemetery.

And so it was one late January day that I was making arrangements for the final rites of a "leaner." I was still new at all this and unskilled in translating the conversation exchanged at such times. I didn't ask enough questions and made too many assumptions, such as "If this funeral is in my church, I'm in charge."

I called our usual organist to see if she was available to play; she wasn't. I called the other woman in the congregation who could play the organ, as we were very blessed to have two people in our little congregation who were musically proficient. Unfortunately, she wasn't available either. I asked my wife, Ruth, to play the piano.

When we arrived at the church, we discovered that there was a choir of "leaners" assembled with the intention of singing "Amazing Grace." I quickly alerted Ruth to that news, and she prepared herself to accompany them, which they didn't know, didn't like, and hadn't requested, because, as I later remembered, Primitive Baptists didn't use instrumental music in their worship. So for them this was a whole new thing.

The service did not get off to a very good start. A little boy about five or six years old whistled through much of the early part of the liturgy; and an elderly man had lost a button off his galluses which he was trying to retrieve. This required that the man get down on his knees and reach up under a pew, while simultaneously explaining to the other worshipers what he was about.

The Primitive Baptist preacher delivered himself of a supra-predestinarian sermon on the God who plans and directs everything that occurs in our lives. He said the day and the time of the death of our neighbor was ordained from before the creation of the world. I had allowed myself to get distracted by the whistling and the search for the lost button, but I was also listening to the sermon, and I wondered if those events were also part of the divine plan for that day, having been ordained from before the creation of the world.

However, what was said by the preacher was, for me, secondary to how he said it. He would shout out a phrase in a litany-like declaration, ending each phrase with a ringing "and–uh"! Then he would suck in his breath and embark on the next pronouncement, which also ended with a rousing, ringing "and–uh"! And so on, and on, and on. And on.

That took a while. And then, it was time for the "leaners" to sing a hymn, with Ruth undertaking an accompaniment on the piano. Ruth played the hymn as it was harmonized in the Methodist hymnal, but the choir of leaners sang it the way they always did: "A-h-mazin-n grace-uh; how-ah suweet-ta thuh-hu ssouwn-duh."

I was seated where I could see Ruth periodically take a quick, quizzical look at the hymnal and then steal a furtive glance at the choir. There was little coherence between what she was playing and what they were singing.

The choir struggled through four verses and sat down. Since at that time it was the custom in our Methodist churches to sing "amen" at the conclusion of a hymn, Ruth played the amen. It was printed right there in the Methodist hymnal.

The choir thought she was starting another verse and got up again. By the time they were up, she was finished. They started randomly sitting down, with the first ones down pulling the others down about them. This is when I remembered that Primitive Baptists used no instrumental music in their worship.

The service had ended, and we began the walk to the cemetery. I was leading the way; the other preacher had stepped away for some reason. As we processed, one of the undertakers asked me for some information to include in the book that was to be given to the family of the deceased. He asked: "Who played the piano?" I answered: "That was my wife, Ruth." And, thinking that he might have wondered why we didn't use the organ, I added: "Neither of our regular organists could be here, so she played the piano."

As I finished speaking, the "leaner" preacher caught up with us to join the procession. All he heard me say was, "Neither of our regular organists could be here, so she played." With feeling, he commented, "Well, I thought that surely wasn't your regular piano-player; she was terrible."

The undertaker just peeled off from the procession and, without another word, disappeared among the gravestones. We finished the service and everybody dispersed, straight and leaner alike. And while I was there, we never did that again.

# Happily Ever After

**E**VERY MORNING AT 2:00 A.M., THE TRAIN CAME roaring through town. Everything shook. The bus station outside my back door shook. And my entire house shook, including the windows and the empty jelly jars I used for drinking glasses and the bed in which I slept.

Sometimes the shades on my bedroom window, stretched down tightly to provide a little modesty shield at night and protection from the early morning sun, would take that rumbling opportunity to let go and retract, flapping wildly. Then my neighbor's dog would bark.

It happened every morning. In our little North Carolina town, the main Southern Railway line between Washington and New Orleans sent trains, passenger and freight, racketing right down the middle of Main Street.

I forgot to tell Ruth.

For a year before we married, I had lived in this big two-story frame parsonage, built circa 1890 and located right there behind the bus station, and after a while I got used to the whole deal—buses pulling in all through the day and night: patrons coming and going from the T-Ville Diner (a streetcar made into a restaurant) and all the people walking up and down my driveway which, for a large segment of the town's population, served as a shortcut to town.

I forgot to tell Ruth about the train.

We married and went to live in my parsonage, which had a wood burning stove in the kitchen, only one closet in the entire house, and no shade on the bathroom window (I hadn't noticed). I forgot to tell her about the 2:00 a.m. train to New Orleans. It always blew its whistle about the time it was running parallel to my house. It was not a bluesy, folksy sound like the trains in country songs; it was more like a battalion of banshees.

We moved in, unpacked some of Ruth's stuff, and settled down to live happily ever after. Which things were—until 2:00 a.m. when that train let out a howl and came charging through our backyard. Ruth shot out of bed, shouting, *"What was that?"*

"Oh," I said, "I forgot to tell you about the train." So I did, and then we settled down to live happily ever after.

It's part of the human condition the way we learn to live with difficulty and inconvenience after a while. We adjust and forget that it is difficult and inconvenient.

Which is an all right thing to do if it is something over which we have no control. We learn to control those things we can, one of which is our attitude about it. The train makes the sound of a category-five hurricane every morning at 2:00 a.m., and there is absolutely nothing one can do about it. You learn to live with it.

But that is not the case of many circumstances by which we claim to be victimized. We do have the power to change things. We are not outmaneuvered by everything that happens. We can take charge of our habits, by God's grace, or of our responses to other people. And in that sense, we are in charge of our future. It doesn't necessarily just happen to us. We can give it shape.

As for that train, we only lived in the house for a year after we married, and a new parsonage was built for our residence in the country, next to one of the four churches to which we had been assigned. The new parsonage was wonderful, and we loved it. But not, of course, until Ruth learned to live with the noise of the wind blowing through the pine trees and the shock of discovering that there was no garbageman.

Then we settled down to live happily ever after.

# Tear Jerkin' and Joy Risin'

TEAR JERKIN' AND JOY RISIN' " IS THE WAY the lady described the worship service that she had attended one night the week before.

She was a member of my congregation and while she never actually said it, the message was delivered that "tear-jerkin' and joy-risin' " was better than the way we did worship at our place. Her husband was more articulate and more urbane than most of the folk of that flock, but he concurred that the service they had experienced was exceptional.

I've attended some worship that I suppose was in that idiom. I did not have my tears jerked, but there were a number of people who seemed to be having a rollicking good time while praising and extolling the name of Jesus. At one particular place of worship, they were eating doughnut holes and drinking cappuccino and whirling around to the music of a five-piece band. I had gone there to preach and walked in after the proceedings were underway only to discover that there was no pulpit. While scouting a place to put my Bible and my notes, I saw the scripture lessons projected on a couple of huge screens along with the hymn texts. The message was clear; there was nothing left to do but throw that Bible down and the notes too, and give myself to the moment.

But, generally speaking, I don't think the current phenomenon known in church circles as "worship and praise" has much of a "tear-jerkin' " component. Not the way it did fifty years ago when the potency of a service of worship was measured by how many people were left in tears at the end of the sermon—perhaps "slain by the Spirit" and piled up at the altar. All crying copiously over their sin.

My friend Marie recounts the story of attending such a service over in west Tennessee in a little church somewhere in the vicinity of Hatchie Bottom and the Mississippi state line. She says one of the ladies was so exuberant in her praise of God that she passed out right there in the church. When some people went to see about her and get her up off the floor, the preacher called out, "Leave her there where Jesus flang her."

That's not done much, anymore. Well, that's not really true; I mean that it's not done much anymore where I go to church. Or for that matter, where you go to church.

My relationship with the lady who reported the worship service that was "tear-jerkin' and joy-risin' " ended when she left the church I pastored before I had been there a year. It was in the spring of 1954, shortly after the U.S. Supreme Court decision was delivered in response to *Brown v. the Board of Education,* a case concerning racial desegregation of the public schools in Little Rock, Arkansas. It was a monumental decision that was to affect all of the United States and, in particular, us in the southern states. I preached a sermon favoring the decision on the next Sunday following its issuance.

After worship, I moved to the door to greet worshipers, and as the lady and her husband presented themselves, I extended my hand, first to her husband and then to her. Neither would shake my hand. The husband said words to me that I don't remember—growly, grumbling words. He looked at me only fleetingly, she not at all. They left and I never saw them again.

That was hard. There was no joy in that moment; not even tears. In that stark encounter, we had stepped into the future.

# Not All Music Is Harmonious

I GREW UP ON A TOBACCO FARM IN KENTUCKY with little or no time or opportunity to plug into American cultural life. The only music I heard was on the radio, at churches, or at the Ballardsville School.

The Ballardsville School was a three-room arrangement that housed about eighty students in grades one through eight. It was there that I made my singing debut at the age of ten, performing "Alexander's Ragtime Band" at the Halloween carnival.

It was also my first experience at public speaking, because the way the program was arranged, when a particular performer finished his gig he was to introduce the next; so I introduced Melvin Cook and Roland Heilman, who played their guitars and sang "Columbus Stockade Blues." Except I didn't know the word *stockade* and I called it something else. In true show-business tradition, they went on and sang "Columbus Stockade Blues."

Another part of my musical training was listening to the radio program *Your Hit Parade* every Saturday night, which played the top ten best-selling records of the previous week. That helped me know what songs I was supposed to like.

The third dimension of my musical exposure was at churches. They all sang pretty much the same songs, but it was done best at the Methodist church because there the piano was played by Miss Christine Goldsborough.

Miss Christine Goldsborough was a born-again Christian who once cornered me at the post office, right in front of the Ten Most Wanted Criminals poster. She asked me my name and then proceeded to give me hers and parsed its meaning in the process. Christine, she said, means "a follower of Christ." Her middle name was Nina, which means "on the way to," and Goldsborough means "the city of gold." She was, therefore, "a follower of Christ on the way to the city of gold." That's what she said, right there in the post office.

Miss Christine played a mean gospel piano. She played what one of my current musical friends calls "hop-along Jesus songs." And she played them better than anybody ever did. I call what she did gospel jazz. It was a combination of stride piano and improvisations on nineteenth- and twentieth-century gospel songs and some early American fuguing tunes. It made you want to get up and do the boogie-woogie. That was a style of dance popular during my high school days. As an aside, I will say somewhat immodestly that Jean Rose Pearce and I did one of the better boogie-woogies in our school.

Miss Christine's gospel jazz made you want to get up and dance. Only you dared not. The main body of religionists in our town were Calvinists. They had all been schooled in

Calvinist ways. Garrison Keillor once said about Calvinists, in whose company he grew up, that "they feared that somewhere out there, somebody was having a good time." And it had to be stopped.

In college I encountered different musical forms, and after I became a pastor, there were all kinds of musical challenges because music was a big part of my work. I often found myself questioned about musical choices that didn't correspond with what the people in my congregations wanted.

In one of my first churches, we were having the Methodist bishop of northern Europe to preach for us, and as I handed out the printed program for the service to the choir, the chief dissident of that congregation, Mrs. W. S. A. Payne, wailed, "I knew it! I knew it! I knew it that on the day when we were having a guest, we'd have some song that nobody ever heard of."

The song was "O for a Thousand Tongues to Sing." Charles Wesley's song, "O, for a Thousand Tongues to Sing." The first song in the book.

Until that moment I had taken her abuse about my elitist tastes in music, but this was too much, and I responded: "I think that if I was as old as you and didn't know 'O for a Thousand Tongues to Sing,' I wouldn't admit it."

I should have known better.

She immediately responded, "Well, I guess if I had all that fancy education at Duke University, I would know everything too."

# Truth's Shadow

I T WAS A LATE AFTERNOON IN EARLY DECEMBER. The telephone rang; Ruth answered; it was a neighbor. Her five-year-old son was a sometime playmate of our five-year-old Joe. The message was that Joe had been telling all the children in our neighborhood that there was no Santa Claus. She thought we should know.

When asked about it, Joe said the report was true; he had said that there is no Santa Claus. He told us that the reason he had said it was that there is no Santa Claus. Which struck me as a fairly logical behavior: that one's statements should issue from a firmly held premise.

We had never discussed that particular subject in our house, so it was an independently held opinion, arrived at on his own. I considered launching into some philosophically inspirational oration, in the manner of Francis Church, when he wrote to Virginia Hanlon in *The New York Sun* in 1897, "Yes, Virginia, there is a Santa Claus." But I looked at Joe's earnest little face and saw that he wasn't to be trifled with, and so I surrendered and said, "That's true, but I would prefer that you didn't feel it necessary to tell all the children in the neighborhood." It was a deal.

The time shifts: The five-year-old was now a six-year-old, and on a summer Sunday afternoon, friends from an earlier parish dropped in for a visit, and brought Joe a book of illustrated Bible stories.

As the adults caught up on one another's lives, Joe took his new book to another room and began poring over it. Shortly, he was back, leaning up against my legs and trying to get my attention: "Daddy—Daddy—Daddy—." I looked down, and he had his new Bible storybook opened to a full-page illustration depicting the prophet Balaam seated on the back of his donkey, stopped in the middle of the road by an angel, who stood with his arms up in the air demanding that Balaam go back whence he had come. The angel had big, feathered wings and a bright aura about his head and face (Numbers 22:22-35).

Joe pointed to the angel and said: "Do you see that? Do you see that?" And when he was sure that he had my attention, he went on: "There is no such thing!" He slammed the book shut and walked away. And all of that was without knowing about the talking donkey.

How does Daddy explain to a six-year-old that he is fast becoming a fundamentalist of the left and that the language of religion is the language of story, poetry, myth, and metaphor? And how does Daddy do it in a tight spot twixt a defiant child who is serving notice that he has ideas of his own and loving, faithful friends who don't even recognize what is happening?

I discovered throughout my career that some of the most interesting people with whom I made contact were people with questions, people who lived uncomfortably with the belief systems of their time and place. People who doubted. People who had the courage to push back some idea that they found disrespectful, to reject some ideology that offended their perception of truth and their sense of admissibility. People, as claimed by Phillip James Bailey in his book *Festus, a Country Town,* "who never doubted, never half believed/Where doubt, there truth is—'tis her shadow."

We need to listen, not only to preachers, philosophers, and professors, but also to poets, playwrights, and storytellers; and sometimes to wise old people, and even to some folk who are restrained under lock and key and are certified by the people in charge as "crazy." It behooves us also to listen to an opinionated five-year-old. God could be speaking.

# A Moral Imagination

THE RULE KEEPERS NO DOUBT MEAN WELL. They want to live lives that make it possible for us to have an ordered society and to honor God. Most organized religions draw up rules for human interaction. In my denomination, we have the rules numbered and add to them a less formalized bunch of resolutions that are up for discussion year in and year out. We know in advance what we ought to do, if not what we will do.

But there is a trap in that kind of morality; it's a shortcut. It doesn't take into account the nuances in any given moment and the range of alternatives that might be open to us.

To travel light morally is strenuous, because it requires the use of the imagination. I think that for myself, who I really am is to be found in the choices I make rather than in the rules I keep. In every moment I am choosing who I am going to be, not what rule I am going to obey.

My children latched on to this early in their lives; it was part of what made Joe march to a different drummer. Which not everybody approves of—it's easier for some people to sing life's song along with you if you will just warble the notes as they are written on the score.

Our daughter, Leslie, was very small and just learning to talk. Often when I dressed her after her bath, we would play a little improvised game of "Beep-Beep." It went like this: I would take my finger and push on her navel as if it were a button and say "beep-beep," and we would both laugh and repeat it again and again.

Ruth said to me one day, "I hope you won't be sorry about teaching that to her." I dismissed her comment as the musing of a soul in bondage to propriety.

Miss Myrtle was a member of our congregation who periodically "dropped in." She didn't come with any purpose; she just "dropped in." Miss Myrtle lived a very circumspect life; she had never married and had never left our little town. Her conversation was mindful and her manner was chaste.

I answered the doorbell one afternoon; it was Miss Myrtle "dropping in." I invited her inside and we both sat down. Soon Ruth joined us, and shortly thereafter Leslie appeared. While Miss Myrtle and I discussed some topic befitting a pastor and a church lady, Leslie posted herself directly in front of our guest. Leslie gathered up her skirt and, facing Miss Myrtle, took her finger, pressed her navel, and said, "Beep-beep."

Miss Myrtle directed her conversation over and around Leslie. She acted as if the child were not there. Leslie wasn't giving up that easily. She just kept on "beeping" Miss

Myrtle until Ruth retrieved her and took her and her beeps somewhere else.

I had taught her how but not when. It's not easy to live with hilarity in a morally imaginative way and at the same time not violate some other person's rules of propriety.

# A Moral Imagination at Work

JOE WAS SEVEN OR EIGHT YEARS OLD WHEN, in an outburst of pique, he hit his fist firmly on the dining room table. He was annoyed about something; he didn't mean to knock seven crystal goblets off the table. They shattered into little bits and slivers, and we parents had a teachable moment. He would have to pay for replacements out of his weekly allowance. As best I recall it, it was going to take a little more than five months.

He was appropriately abashed and humbly gave assent to his punishment. It was important, we thought, that children should learn that actions issue in consequences. One gets to act, but one doesn't always get to choose the consequences of that act. This is stuff right out of a moral philosophy that even seven- or eight-year-olds can understand—must understand. In this case, his explosive anger had resulted in the destruction of some valued crystal stemware, and therefore he should have to make some personal sacrifice to replace them.

Things went well, but several weeks into his chastening, I noticed that he had new comic books and an occasional new toy automobile. I asked him where he got the money for his purchases, and he guilelessly answered that his sister had been giving him money. We checked that story and it was true. Each week she was splitting her allowance with him, right down the middle. Half for him, half for herself.

Oh, my!

I had been so bent on teaching consequences and responsibility that I had missed out on this really religious thing that was going on in my house. I had failed to see this sacramental thing that was happening between the little ones, the least ones in our house—acts of grace on the part of them both, the giver and the receiver.

# Forgiveness

**A**S HE LEARNED TO ASSERT HIMSELF WITHIN the culture at large, Joe would at times mix it up with me. There was no particular subject nor set of subjects that would stir up in him strong negative feelings; nonetheless, he found it necessary to defy my ruling on this or that. And he would not be dissuaded.

I was raised in the home of a nineteenth-century man, a man who was an adult by the time the century turned in 1900. He was one of twelve children in the family, and there were strict rules for maintaining order in that house, and the identity of the commanding officer was never disputed. It was my grandfather. My father learned parenting from him.

In my father's house, there was no negotiation of the rules, and no excuses were accepted for failed responsibilities. Punishment was swift.

All of which is about this: I did not have good parenting skills. Particularly, I did not know how to deal with Joe's strong spirit, which sometimes issued in defiance. So the thing I would do was to blow myself up BIG—get loud, and crush his little self. As I had been spanked, I spanked, even though I once heard a friend say, "Never hit a child except in anger; there is no other excuse for it."

One night it ended. I don't remember the cause. But I do remember, with wrenching remorse, the outcome. I had spanked Joe; I hit him and told him to go to bed. He did.

And then I was overcome by contrition—regret and penitence. I reproached myself: "You just beat up a child. You just beat up a child." I went back into his darkened room and sat on the edge of his bed, and I confessed to him: "I'm sorry. I'm really sorry. I should not have done that. I'm sorry."

And he said back to me, in the dark: "That's OK, Daddy; that's OK."

I said, "No, Joe, it's not OK!" I felt a visceral pain, like having been hit in the stomach. I went on: "But thank you; I am really sorry."

To be forgiven the unforgivable is to be disassembled and put back together again—reconstituted.

# A Gun and a Bottle of Gin

I HAD JUST COME IN FROM A MEETING. IT WAS about ten o'clock at night. My neighbor Archie called and said he wanted to talk with me. In a matter of moments, I saw him drive into the driveway, and according to our agreement I went out to the car to meet him.

He had received a call from an acquaintance, a man named Lefty, who told Archie that he had discovered that his wife was pregnant by another man. Lefty was going to kill her and himself. Lefty knew his friend Archie was a faithful man, and he wanted Archie to come pray for them before he did that. Archie wanted me to go with him. I agreed.

When we walked in, Lefty's wife was sitting up on the bed, reclining against a couple of pillows with her legs stretched out in front of her. Lefty sat on the edge of the bed turned toward her, with a gun in one hand and a bottle of gin in the other.

He was furious with her, and he said he was going to shoot her and then himself. I asked him for the details of why, and he spun them out. I kept talking and asking questions—trying to buy time. He urged me to get on with the prayer, and then he would proceed with his plan.

In retrospect, this story sounds as if I knew what I was doing. I didn't. I was extemporizing. If we ever covered anything like this in pastoral care classes, I wasn't paying attention.

Many years later, Ruth and I, along with our college-age children, were visiting London. We went one night to see a farcical play, "Donkeys' Years" by Michael Frayn. It concerned a  twenty-fifth-year university class reunion. One of the returning alumni had become a Church of England priest. When another alumna  crawled out onto a high-up ledge with the announced intention of jumping and killing herself, others sent for the priest. Perhaps he would know what to do.

When he received the summons, the priest responded with great anguish that he didn't know what to do; he said he didn't "do ledges." As a matter of fact, he had cut class the day they did ledges. That's the way I felt that night in Lefty's house, although at the time there was nothing even slightly amusing about it.

For some reason, Lefty asked Archie to leave, and Archie went out to the car and waited there. I am sure that Archie prayed earnestly for his pastor and for Lefty and his wife as well.

During all of that querying on my part, Lefty revealed his fear that killing his wife and himself might mean that he would go to hell. I assured him that he would; he would just have to decide if killing her was worth that.

I wasn't at all sure that what I was saying was true, and it certainly wasn't anything we discussed in seminary, but I didn't choose this topic. Lefty did. I decided that our divinity school equivocations about hell not necessarily being a place, just somewhere that God isn't, were a little too abstract for this occasion. So I went with Lefty's understanding, exploiting his fear of fiery furnaces and other Dante-esque imagery. After all, a pair of lives were at stake here; maybe three. Fortunately, that thought about three lives in danger didn't occur to me until the next morning.

We talked on about death and hell, and periodically I would pick up the gin bottle and hand it to him. He would take a swig and put it down. It occurred to me that if he kept drinking that gin straight out of the bottle, he would eventually get so drunk that perhaps I could get the gun away from him.

Time crawled by. After a while, I realized that it was after midnight and that Lefty was getting more confused in his speech and drinking more gin and that he probably didn't want to kill his wife anyway—that this was all a piece of outrageous theater. I began to think that this was going to work. If I just took my time, I could probably get the gun. Once I saw him lay it down, but he picked it up again. And then he put it down again; his speech growing more and more unintelligible.

About one o'clock, he fell asleep. I took the gun and went to the door and motioned for Archie to come in. Lefty's wife got off the bed and left in a pickup truck. We positioned Lefty on the bed, turned out the lights, and departed with the gun.

Back home in my own bed, I finally got around to praying for Lefty and his wife, and I thanked God for Archie, who cared about his friend. I included a little addendum to my prayer: "And thank you, God, for that bottle of gin."

# Acts of Grace

IN THOSE EARLY PARISHES, IT WAS STILL customary to have a guest preacher come and deliver a series of sermons that dealt largely with personal holiness, and with repentance and grace. These were revival meetings of a sort, only not protracted as they once had been over the period of a couple of weeks.

Part of the proceedings was to invite the pastor and his wife and the visiting preacher to dinner at the homes of different members of the congregation. Only we called it supper in those places. Dinner was a midday meal, the big meal of the day. It was a hearty repast, because the farmers were in the middle of their workday.

So when it came time to have the "revival," it was also a time to go into the homes of the flock and to eat wondrously. And along the way, there were also equally remarkable.

At one noonday meal, the head of the house, a tobacco farmer, was not as impressed with his dinner guests as was his wife, who had invited the guest preacher, Ruth, and me. As a matter of fact, the farmer was a bit cranky, and as soon as the meal had progressed through about a dozen courses, but before the dessert came, he pushed his chair back, reached into the bib of his overalls, and took out a package of cigarettes.

He put one to his lips and lit up. Then he inhaled and blew a big puff of smoke toward the guest preacher, an older man who was both fearless and fearsome. The farmer hadn't been to hear the sermon, and he had no idea what he was heading into when he threw down the gauntlet: "Preacher, you and your brethren are always talking about the evils of smoking. Exactly, what is bad about smoking?"

"Well, I tell you one thing, brother," said the old preacher. "You'd smell a heap better if you didn't smoke."

There were other arresting statements, some of which we never unriddled, such as the time during revival meetings when we went for supper at the home of Mattie and Marshall. Mattie had prepared a banquet: there were three different meats, eight or ten vegetables, and three or four desserts, not counting The Cake.

The Cake had a story that went with it. Mattie came into the room carrying what appeared to have started out as a cake and then had suffered great travail in its birthing. It looked as if someone had stepped on it, not in the middle but on one side. As she came through the door on her way to the table, Mattie was talking about The Cake.

She said, "I don't know what happened to this cake; I took it upstairs and put it in a lard can, but it still did this."

That thing about The Cake fell into the same category as a thing said by another of our hostesses, who was apologizing about her meal when she announced, "I was going to have green beans, but I didn't have any corn."

Most of these splendid meals began with a disclaimer on the part of the host or hostess. Not all, however, were as cryptic as the lady who wanted to serve green beans but couldn't because she had no corn, nor as confounding as Mattie's explanation of what happened to The Cake.

There were pleadings such as, "Take out and help yourself. If we can eat this seven days a week, surely you can eat it one." The husband might pass a delectable dish and offer an apology such as, "We've had so much rain, the tomatoes have developed some kind of mold" or "This is a new hybrid corn, and I haven't decided whether I like it or not."

One host expressed dissatisfaction with the country ham, baked just right and with those little white spots that indicate that it is at least two years old—the food of the gods to me. After about the third such protestation, I decided that he wasn't getting the response he desired, and I said, "Mr. Paul, this ham is so good that I don't want to go to heaven if it's not there."

There was a considerable silence. Then Mr. Paul said, "Russell, you know there will be no country ham in heaven."

I stumbled around to cover up that remark with some reference to how much I enjoyed country ham that had to be at least two years old to be as good as this, and gradually the conversation started up again. But every now and then, Mr. Paul would stop the talk and say, "Russell, I just can't believe what you said about not wanting to go to heaven if there is no country ham there. You know there will be no country ham in heaven."

And my response would be some version of, "Right! There will be no country ham in heaven.... That was a really stupid thing for me to say.... I was trying to be funny but that's not very funny, is it?... Of course that's not funny because we all know there will be no baked country ham in heaven ... not in heaven, no baked ham there. Ever."

I sat down often to what amounted to feasts, consisting of food that my hosts had grown, harvested, and prepared. I came to appreciate what that meant. They were pleased with what they had to offer, but their modesty made them demur; required them to apologize. Many of the women thought themselves without skills. These were the same women who, when I announced that I was going to marry, set about doing all sorts of intricate needlework on sheets, pillowcases, and tablecloths with which our home was hallowed.

The men brought garden produce and left it on the back porch to be found when we got up in the morning. And they brought chickens and pork and beef that they had just slaughtered.

On one occasion when I visited a member, he gave me four slices of cured ham cut right out of the middle of the ham. I took it home and went immediately to the kitchen. Pearl was there. She was a friend of ours who came weekly to help clean up the house and mind our baby.

I took the ham to the counter where Pearl was working and, without saying a word, put the package down and unwrapped it and fanned out the slices so that she might get a better view of my astonishing gift. She took a quick look and without even changing her expression said, "I'll tell you this, Reverend, there ain't much preaching going on around here."

All of those gifts were acts of grace that I finally learned to acknowledge without revealing my own sense of unworthiness—without insolence or impudence.

# The Chicken

AT MY FIRST PARISH, IT WAS EXPECTED THAT the preacher visit all the parishioners some time or other, and, as many of them did not yet have telephones and were working at home, the preacher just dropped by.

The parishioners' largesse often demanded that some gift or other be pressed on me as I departed. I arrived at that first parish about the first of October, and at some gathering where the parishioners brought covered dishes I tasted my first persimmon pie. I grew up on a farm, but I had never heard of or seen such a thing. Persimmons I knew—they grew wild in the fence rows, and the fruit was bitterly astringent until the first fall frost rendered them edible.

I was offered some of that first persimmon pie by one of the ladies of the parish. She had baked and brought it. Fearing that my face might lapse into a perpetual pucker, but fearing more her deep offense if I refused, I took a piece and tasted it and it was good. I was so relieved, I was a little too effusive in my appreciation, and the word spread that the new preacher liked persimmon pie. The message was, "He likes it a lot."

One morning shortly thereafter, I opened my refrigerator door to take an inventory, and there was a half-empty carton of milk and nine persimmon pies.

One day after Ruth and I married, as I was leaving the farm home of a member, the lady told me to wait a minute; she had something for me. She said that she would meet me at my car, where she gave me a live chicken with its feet tied together. I thanked her and went directly home, parked my car, and took the chicken in the house to Ruth.

Ruth was startled. "What are we going to do with that?" she asked. I said that we were going to kill it and eat it. She advised that we weren't going to do that right at suppertime, and that I should put it in the garage. She said, "Maybe it will get away before morning."

I went early to the garage the next day; it was about 7:00 a.m. The chicken was still there. So we planned a strategy. I had seen my mother clean a chicken, and it had sometimes been my job to kill the chicken. I knew how to do that, and so I did.

It was the next step that wasn't familiar. I had seen Mama put the newly killed chicken into hot water and then remove it and pluck the feathers. That was kind of vaguely reminiscent. So I boiled the water, put the chicken in for too long a time, and as I plucked the chicken some of the flesh came off with the feathers. This wasn't going well.

I went out onto the porch, cut the chicken open, and prepared to take out the entrails, but I didn't even know where to start. So I handed *The Joy of Cooking* (a wedding gift cookbook) to Ruth to read and pass on to me how this operation was to proceed. She read something about taking hold of something and pulling it out. I had my hand inside the chicken, and I asked her, "Does it say anything about how it feels?"

Periodically, this routine became too unpleasant for Ruth, and she had to run in the house, leaving me to figure the thing out by myself. It took us four hours, and by that time rigor mortis had set in and the chicken's legs were stiff and the whole thing was pretty disgusting. So we decided to put the chicken in the freezer compartment of the refrigerator and give ourselves some time to forget about it.

Now and then over the following weeks, the topic of the chicken would come up. Were we ready to eat it? We were not. We never did.

The gracious lady who gave us the chicken told me sometime later to come back to her house; she had two more chickens for us. Ruth and I couldn't even imagine going through that again, so I would go out of my way not to drive by the lady's house. I was afraid she might see me and wonder why I didn't stop. I would sometimes drive eight or ten miles out of my way in order not to pass that way.

Time finally tripped me up. She and I were face to face, and she said, "You never have come by to get those chickens." It was said as a declarative sentence, but it had a little implied question mark at the end. "Why don't you come by this afternoon and get them?"

I decided to be straight-up with her, and I said, "I can't do that today. I don't have the time to do that. It takes me longer than a while—tto do that."

She responded, "Don't even think about doing it yourself; there's a poultry house right on the edge of town that you will pass on your way home. They will dress those chickens for ten cents each."

# The Parable of the Taxi Driver

IN BIG JAPANESE CITIES, THE TAXI DRIVERS wear white hats and white gloves. The backs of the seats are covered with white lace doilies. In some taxis, there are little white lace-covered boxes of tissues up in the back window. When the driver has no fare, he gets out a big feather duster and brushes away the tiniest speck that may fall upon the exterior of the car.

You should not let the ambience fool you, however. All the taxi drivers in Tokyo and Osaka drive as if they were former kamikaze pilots. I finally convinced myself that the only way to keep my blood pressure in check and my hair on straight was never to look through the front windshield. That way, I wouldn't know what we were nearly hitting, either in the middle of the street or up on the sidewalk.

Many of you have ridden in New York taxis which do not have lace doilies. There, the driver had better not get caught wearing white gloves or his friends will beat him up. The last three New York taxi drivers I had were a Croatian, a Nigerian, and a turbaned Sikh from northern India. Among all of them they knew only three things to say in the English language: "Yes, "No," and "That will be forty dollars."

In my hometown, the last taxi ride I had was in a vehicle of undetermined vintage that was last washed in 1991. The driver looked like a linebacker for the Pittsburgh Steelers; she had a gold front tooth and called me "honey" all the way to town.

And there was Iqbar, our driver in Hyderabad, India, who took us wherever we wanted to go, then sat in the unrelenting heat and waited for us. For eight dollars a day!

I like to think about such people and wonder what their private lives are like. I look at the Japanese driver, with his ramrod posture, his inscrutable face, and his taxi that looks like a boudoir, and I wonder what he does at home. I look at those displaced persons who drive taxis in New York, and I wonder what their careers were in their birth countries and what was so terrible that made them leave. I see that affable woman who tosses luggage like a stevedore, and I wonder how she ended up doing that. Elegant Iqbar, darkly handsome, during several days with us said one personal thing— that his children had just passed their university entrance exams. It was printed in the morning paper, and he showed the paper to us.

And for all the differences among those drivers, their stories are not much different from ours. They are people trying to make it. Going to places they have never been before; they don't really want to go; it is someone else's destination.

Sometimes they wind down back alleys and through almost impassable traffic. Sometimes they go against the traffic, looking for opportunities to get in, get out. Collecting fares and moving on.

We tend to pass one another without noticing or being noticed because we all have so much to tend to in our own lives that we really don't have time to stop and consider the lives of anonymous others. It is the parable of the taxi driver.

# The Real World

**A**RTHUR IS A SOMETIMES COLLEGE INSTRUCTOR of English who wanders back and forth between reality and illusion. He is gentle and kind and never willfully offends anyone, but now and then his behavior is so unusual that somebody hies him to the hospital.

I went to visit him there, feeling anxious about the impending encounter. As I turned a corner on my way toward Arthur's room, I could make out a group of three or four persons around a low table right in the middle of the corridor.

When I got closer, I could see that it was Arthur and some other "bunkies," also known as patients. Arthur had rousted up a table and covered it with a brightly colored cloth. He was having a tea party for anybody who wanted to attend. I was invited, and so I sat down, feeling a little apprehension. I should have had none.

It was a splendid party.

Arthur recited from memory long passages of nineteenth-century English poetry with artful declamation. While we sipped our tea, others began to make offerings of stories remembered, or anecdotes from their personal lives.

Only one of them didn't seem to be enjoying the occasion. He had a red button in his hand, into which he kept speaking cryptic messages; he said it was a remote microphone. He also received messages on it. Sensing his anxiety, Arthur and the others told him not to worry about those people and their calls. Nobody said that it was only a plastic button with four little holes in the middle. They urged him just to hang up on those people and enjoy all the lovely things that were happening. "And if they call back, just tell them you are busy."

They were interesting and amusing people. The tempo picked up. Two nurses joined us. I hated leaving when the time came to go.

I was escorted out through locked doors, got on the elevator, and rode down to the main lobby, where two large, aggressive ladies elbowed their way on while I was trying to get off. Out front, a man was sitting in the drop-off lane blowing his horn because some unauthorized driver had parked there. That night I attended a meeting at the church, where at least a half-dozen people were confident that communists were writing our denominational Sunday school curriculum. They had catalogued a number of references to the poor and had underlined suggestions that as we cared for the disadvantaged, we served God. It took a while, but we decided that it probably had not been imposed on us by the communists.

I got home in time for the news, which gave me the latest American body count from the war that was raging in Southeast Asia.

As I lay my head on the pillow that night, I thanked God for Arthur and his sweet little band of "bunkies," for it was among them that I had found solace and peace.

# Talking the Faith

IN SOME WAYS, THERE IS AN UPSIDE TO NOT being raised in the church: There's not as much remedial work to be done as one reaches college age and then charges into the fray of life in the real world.

For a while in the late 1970s, I was pastor of the American Protestant Church in Bonn, Germany. We shared a building with the American Roman Catholic Church. While we were having Sunday school at 10:00 a.m., the Catholic congregation was celebrating the mass, and then at 11:00 a.m. the two groups swapped spaces and we had worship. The Protestant church had a single adult Bible study group during the Sunday school hour that met at the nearby American Embassy Club, because there was no church space big enough to accommodate the Catholic mass and all the Sunday school groups.

That Bible study group was a remarkable mix of people from a broad spectrum of Christian traditions and none. There were as many as twenty-six nationalities. They were people of such diverse linguistic, educational, and sociopolitical backgrounds that the hour demanded from me something like a high-wire balancing act as I looked for a language that conveyed what I was trying to say.

I discovered early on that my southern American English locution and lingo hindered my being understood. One British lady said to me following worship one Sunday morning, "I have difficulty understanding you; you are so, so-o-o American." Consequently, I worked assiduously to put the consonants back in my speech and to pronounce every syllable (as the Germans do) which got me into trouble when I returned to the American South.

When I did return, after about the third Sunday of worship in our new parish, Ruth said to me as we made our way home, "It's time to cool the consonants. You're home, and your enunciation sounds affected." I tried, but evidently I wasn't making as much headway as I thought, because soon I received a letter from a member of the congregation who was put off by my pronunciation of the word *often*. I pronounced the *t*, saying "off-ten." She wanted me to stop it; it annoyed her.

That critique occasioned a reflection on my part of just how my way of talking had evolved over the years—just how far I had come from my old Kentucky home. I recalled a high school experience when the principal, who addressed all the girls as "Miss Lady" and all the boys as "Mr. Man," said to me: "Mr. Man, (pause), you have a lazy tongue."

It took me a while to understand the meaning of that sentence. Then I realized he was criticizing my speech—the way I softened hard consonants; the way I dropped final *t's, d's,* and *g's*; and the way I said "warsh-rag" for washcloth, "scu me" for excuse me, and "idden id" instead of isn't it.

I made it through what passed for our town's high school (which actually was called Funk Seminary) and went on to a small but good college (the right place for me), and on about the third day on campus I went to try out for a singing group, an auditioned *a capella* choir. After some talk about why I wanted to belong to the group (I liked the sound they made) and what experience I had (none), the professor turned to the piano, ran a few arpeggios, and said, "OK, *Kintucky,* let's see what you can do."

There it was again; someone was making fun of the way I talked. And I determined right then that I would refine my speech.

A long time later, there I was every Sunday morning in the American Embassy Club in Bonn, Germany, leading an interdenominational, multinational, multilingual study of the Bible.

There was one seriously thoughtful Swiss man, who sat with his French language Bible open on one knee and his Greek New Testament open on the other. *He was intimidating.* There were devout American evangelical Christians with huge amounts of Scripture committed to memory and no doubts or questions about their faith. *They were intimidating.* There were also some employees of multinational corporations posted in nearby towns who had never before read the Bible but simply were looking for English-speaking company. More than occasionally, one of these individuals talked to me quietly after class, asking me for help locating the particular passage we were discussing by saying whether it was in the front, middle, or back of the Bible. They would say, "Don't assume that we know where the passage is, or for that matter how it is spelled." *I was intimidated* by their utter dependence on me as the teacher.

I listened. The ideas were as varied as the group members, and often the best learning and most challenging ideas came from the people for whom Bible study was an entirely new experience. As trust built, the minds of the participants with the least accumulated dogma were often the first ones to disentangle their ideas about how we may expect to encounter God. They weren't required to accommodate a generally accepted orthodoxy. They were free to say what they felt like saying.

Years later, back in the U.S., I was part of a group of men who regularly came together early one weekday morning in order to wrestle with the preacher's text for the following Sunday. As a group, these men were no less diverse in their knowledge and understanding of Scripture than my Bonn class.

One particular Advent Tuesday morning, we were trying

to work out a satisfactory group understanding of the Greek word *logos,* as all students of the New Testament must if they are to understand the evangelist John's use of that word as he describes the Christ:

In the beginning was the Word (logos)

And the Word was with God, and the Word was God.

He was in the beginning with God.

All things came into being through him, and without him not one thing came into being.

What has come into being in him was life, and the life was the light of all people.

The light shines in the darkness, and the darkness did

not overcome it. (John 1:1-5)

There were about twenty-five of us there, and most of the ones taking part in the discussion were presenting varying versions of what biblical scholarship has been proposing for generations when one man quietly offered, and somewhat apologetically: "How about 'in the beginning was the DNA?'"

Yeah, how about that?

"Mr. Man," you instantaneously made us think differently than we had about one of the seminal concepts of our faith. We had to take an age-old faith statement and focus it through a mid-twentieth-century discovery.

At every turn in my career, there were such new

challenges, new stories, a unique understanding of the human situation. I wish I had been wiser, less pedantic, more accessible, less sure of myself (more sure of myself). I believed too many things. I wish I hadn't talked so much and had done more listening.

# That's What Friends Are For

IN RETROSPECT, I THINK THAT I WAS NOT A good friend to many. I had a great many acquaintances, and I shared a lot of life with a number of them, but there was always something held back on my part. Something restrained. I regret that.

However, now and then I would find a friend who was not very much like the people with whom I typically associated. Such people were often larger than life—amusing, *outre* people. They didn't keep the conventions of the culture in which I lived, nor did we share many common values. They gave me access to parallel universes. They made me laugh and often at myself. That was my problem; I never minded my preaching responsibilities, but I didn't like being The Preacher. These people were totally unimpressed, favorably or unfavorably, with The Preacher.

Hugo was one of those friends. Hugo came to the United States as a foreign exchange college student. He grew up Roman Catholic in Ecuador, and after he finished college he went to the Wharton School of Business in Pennsylvania on his way to working as a stockbroker. He didn't have a lot of use for priests or preachers. But we became friends because neither of us was beholden to the other in any way.

One year, I took a group of high school and college students to work in Guatemala rebuilding homes after a devastating earthquake. It was in March; the students were on spring break. I asked Hugo if he would go with us and act as translator. He agreed.

He was short and dark and wore a sailor's hat turned down over his big expressive eyes. He moved very rapidly and had a smile as warming as the morning sun. He kept us all entertained with his malapropisms. Once he was trying to express his anxiety and stated that he was on "needles and threads." At another time he talked about going to visit a friend to see if it were possible that his friend might sell him some North Carolina mountain property. He mused that, when he got back to the States, he was going to his friend and "feel him around" about that possibility.

Hugo arrived up on the side of the volcano where we camped with only three cigarettes left in a package. He had failed to buy some en route. One of the high school girls had a pack with her, and he kept bumming cigarettes from her. Every morning, we all woke up to the sound of Hugo going from tent to tent, calling in a loud stage whisper, "Cigarette lady! Cigarette lady!" He never could remember her name nor which tent was hers, and consequently that was the wakeup call to all of us each morning.

Hugo's most memorable exchange came near the end of one workday in that mountainous part of Guatemala. Leslie, Randy, and I had been assigned to take the roof off of a small adobe brick house, in preparation for the installation of a tin roof that was to go on in place of a traditional one of stacked loose tiles.

An earthquake had come in the early morning hours while the people of that region slept. The tiles had been jarred loose, and at this house the husband had been killed by falling tiles. His two small children and his wife, no more than twenty years old, survived.

Our workday had ended, and the three of us were very tired as we walked along a dusty road on our way back to our camp. We rounded a curve and there was Hugo. He motioned toward a small group of men standing about a hundred yards away. He said they had heard that there was a priest in our group. No priest had come to their village since the quake. They wanted to find the priest and ask for a blessing.

Through weary eyes, I looked intently at him and said, "Hugo, I'm a Methodist; I can't do that!"

He grasped my arm and spoke very deliberately: "They don't even know what the hell a Methodist is. You go over there and give them a blessing!" And he pushed me in their direction.

As I approached these short, compact men, descendants

of the ancient Maya, they all removed their wide-brimmed straw hats and clutching them to their chests in one synchronized motion, bowed their heads, and fell to their knees in the tall grass.

I couldn't remember how to do the sign of the cross—whether you started with the vertical line of the cross or the horizontal line. So I fumbled through a funky little sign of the cross and said: "The blessing of almighty God—Father, Son, and Holy Spirit—be with you always. Amen." And they all responded, "Amen."

It was an intensely sweet moment. Later, I looked for Hugo in order to thank him for insisting that I do that, but he was preoccupied. He couldn't find the cigarette lady.

# Beyond the Pale

I N MY SECOND PARISH, WHICH WAS LOCATED in a fairly taut little college town, presided over by some seriously Presbyterian religionists, there wasn't a lot of laughing going on. In addition to that, I was considered an outsider and as a result was treated somewhat diffidently by the townsfolk.

One night, at a dinner party, I was seated next to a rather elegant lady of the town with whom I was not previously acquainted. We talked about a lot of subjects, and as those things go it wasn't a negative experience. We both did our part.

After dinner, we rose from the table to go to the living room for coffee. I helped her with her chair, and while I was sliding it back to the table she expressed her pleasure at having met me, and tagged that pleasantry with this: "It is nice to know you. In the little town in Virginia where I grew up, Methodists weren't very nice people."

I then proved her assessment of Methodists on target by responding: "That's interesting, because there were no Presbyterians in the little town in Kentucky where I grew up. There was a little vacant church building there, commonly known as the Presbyterian church; it had been abandoned by the Presbyterians some years previous. I suppose according to some divine plan."

That little college town was where my pastor predecessor suggested that I join the Lions Club, the only civic club in town. It met in my church; the meal was prepared by the ladies of my congregation. My predecessor said that he hadn't joined the club and he felt that was a mistake; he recommended that I become a member.

Ruth and I talked about it and did the numbers on the cost of joining, and we decided that it would be close but I should join. I didn't, however, because they never invited me.

As time passed, I ran up on some other marginal people like myself who lived out there beyond the pale. One was George, the college chaplain, and another was an Episcopal priest, Ben, a young cleric in his first parish. His was a mission parish attached to another church nearby. Ben spent a lot of his time just trying to flush some Anglican communicants out of the surrounding countryside. There were only twenty people on the roll of his little mission church.

One fall, there was a new commanding officer assigned to the ROTC at the local college—Colonel Jefferson, an attractive, urbane man who had six children. There was Episcopalianism somewhere in his pedigree, and in our town you had to identify yourself quickly or find yourself co-opted by the Calvinists. Colonel Jefferson decided to identify himself with the Episcopal mission and set out to have all his children baptized at once, something he had previously foregone.

Late one Sunday afternoon, my doorbell rang and it was Ben, the Episcopalian. He was harried-looking and in a bother: "I need some coffee. Make some coffee! I have just baptized all six of Colonel Jefferson's children in a single ceremony, from the oldest to the youngest. It went well until we got to the second from the last. He wouldn't let anybody hold him and he wouldn't stay still. He was running all around the church whooping and dodging the older children who were trying to catch him. I went on and baptized the youngest one, and finally the wild one made a run by me, and I put my hand in the baptismal font, got a handful of water, and threw it at him as he passed, declaring, 'I baptize you in the name of the Father, and of the Son, and of the Holy Spirit.' I have never before baptized a child on the run."

I said, "It probably has never been done before. Ben, this is big, really big. We need to get this written down somewhere, like in *The Domesday Book* (authorized by William the Conqueror in 1068) or Ripley's *Believe It or Not*." He was not amused. But he remembered.

# Ben, the Episcopalian

I N OUR LITTLE TOWN OF 2,400 RESIDENTS (including 1,000 college students), there were seven Christian churches. Only now and then did one congregation intersect with another. I reference one of those occasions here. There was a service of some ecumenical sort held in the Episcopal church. Ben, the Episcopalian, was in charge; I was to read the lessons. Ben was in full regalia. He wore a black cassock, a white surplice over that, a cross on a heavy chain, a stole, and an academic hood. I was in my usual mufti. I had not yet affected ecclesiastical garb. I mostly wore a greenish suit with a shiny seat and matching elbows. One of the congregants finally got up his nerve and told me to get a new suit. I did, and it was a deep navy blue; the jacket had a red satin lining. It was great for Pentecost.

That night at the ecumenical service, just prior to the processional hymn, Ben opened a door slightly and pointed out, in the chancel area, a chair where I was to sit. He said, "Just stand in front of it until the processional hymn ends, and then be seated there."

I did as directed, marched in, and stood in front of my designated seat while enthusiastically singing the hymn, but

I was almost immediately distracted by the antics of Martha Ann Derryberry, a well-known community leader and pillar of the Episcopal church. She was obviously distressed by something that was happening in the chancel area.

She would whisper to her husband on one side of her and to her neighbor on the other side and once turned all the way around to discuss the matter with the two ladies behind her. The longer it went on, I could tell it somehow involved me. I surreptitiously checked my zipper and wiped the back of my hand across my mouth, lest I had some leftover remnants of supper there.

The hymn ended, and I sat. As I was going down, Martha Ann did an audible intake of breath that increased in volume the closer my sitter got to the petit-pointed seat of the chair. She was in a near state of incapacitation by the time I had firmly sat.

When the service ended, Martha Ann made a beeline for me and informed me that I had sat in "The Bishop's Chair" and that no one ever sat in "The Bishop's Chair" except the bishop on his occasional visits to the church. I profusely apologized and kept walking while Martha Ann examined the chair to be sure it had not been permanently defiled.

When I got back to Ben's office, he was taking off his vestments. I told him of my encounter with Martha Ann, and he said without even turning around, "In the first place,

Russell, Martha Ann used to be a Methodist, and there is no Episcopalian more zealous than a former Methodist; and second, what you did was a real violation of protocol. You should not have sat there."

"Ben," I said, "you told me to sit there; you pointed out the chair to me. You said stand in front of that chair until we finish the processional hymn, and then sit in it. So, I sat in it. "

Ben responded, "We'll have to write this down somewhere, I mean so we don't make that mistake again." He had remembered.

# George, the Chaplain

GEORGE, THE COLLEGE CHAPLAIN FROM OUT there beyond the pale with Ben, the Episcopalian, was a friend who kept me lucid. I enjoyed George's sardonic wit and ironic speech, especially when he turned it on church people and institutions. In a way, George, Ben, and I all lived on the edge of the prevailing culture of our town, enjoying front-row seats at the circus and passing judgments on what we saw there—pretending to be in it, but not of it.

George once described the architectural style of a major church in the Texas oil town where he grew up as being "bastard Byzantine with leaking Queen Anne turrets" and the lady who played the massive organ there as getting all her incidental service music out of a book entitled *Fifty Snappy Organ Preludes and Postludes.*

My mother was not a very good cook; as a matter of fact, some of her stuff was barely edible. She cooked cabbage until it turned pink, green beans until they turned black, and all her fried eggs had a flounce of brown lace. But Mama could make a longed-for chocolate pie.

My wife, Ruth, had two small children, a house to look after, a Sunday school class to teach, the church's Women's

Society of Christian Service in which to participate, her book club and the telephone to answer. I had no secretary. I was left to understand that if I wanted a chocolate pie, the kitchen was "that way." She pointed.

One Sunday night, I set upon a new career—as the maker of chocolate pies. I mixed up the pie according to a recipe I found somewhere. I don't remember much about how it was made. It had in it sugar and eggs and chocolate, of course, and while it didn't seem to be coming together very well, I was hopeful.

I didn't realize that you were supposed to cook the pie before you put the meringue on, and that probably contributed to the unfortunate outcome. Also, I didn't know that when you made the meringue, you beat the egg whites with the sugar but you didn't dump in all the sugar at once. You put it in a small amount at a time. Who knew?

Having completed all the steps, I put the pie in the oven and happily anticipated magic. After an appropriate length of time, I opened the oven and took out the pie. It was a disaster. It just sloshed around in the pan, and the meringue was mucus-like with a little pile of bubbles on top, right in the middle.

About that time, George rang the doorbell and Ruth ushered him in. Unbeknownst to me, she instructed him to go immediately to the kitchen, where "Russ is making a chocolate pie."

George walked into the kitchen just as I took the pie from the oven. I didn't see him; I was so dumbstruck, staring at the pie, wondering where I had gone wrong.

I wasn't even aware of his presence until he said, "Who spit on your pie?"

# Hans, the German

**H**ANS WAS GERMAN, A BIG GUY WHO PLAYED on a championship handball team in his early years. That's handball played on a field, not the kind where you bounce the ball against a wall.

He had a big voice and a loud cascading laugh that started as a giggle but evolved into a deep rumble. He was fifteen years old when World War II ended with the suicide death of Adolf Hitler. His father was an officer in the German army; his mother was an independent thinker, and she regularly listened to the BBC radio, which was considered a disloyal act. Hans was a member of the Hitler Youth, and late in the war, as a very young teenager, he was sent to northern Germany to fill sandbags.

When Hans returned, he discovered that his home had been destroyed by Allied planes. His mother had painted on a retaining wall the name of a neighboring Rhine River town where she could be found. Hans joined her there, and soon the American army reached the west bank of the river and set up fortifications. The German army was dug in on the other side, trying to keep the Allied armies from crossing the Rhine.

It was a hellish time. Hans reported seeing a German soldier on the other side of the river shot off his motorcycle early one day. He said that he watched all through the day to see if anyone would come pick up the soldier. No one came; he lay there until after dark. Hans assumed that he died there.

Hans had a big vibrant personality to go with his six-foot-five-inch body. In our first conversation, we discovered that we were the same age, and we briefly shared stories of our time growing up in enemy countries.

On the occasion of my fiftieth birthday, I was at work in my office at the American Protestant Church of Bonn, Germany, where I was pastor. The building was open; the door to my office was not. There came a very loud knock on the door and I got up to answer it. I opened the door and there stood Hans. He had two glasses in one hand and a bottle of sekt (the German equivalent of champagne) in the other. He announced in a big voice, "Ruzzell, today together we are one hundred years old!" It was a great birthday surprise. It had been a hard year adjusting to a new language and a new culture. Probably the most difficult adjustment had been learning to live in the diplomatic community, where everything was highly structured, layered with protocol, and defined by abstraction.

Hans made me laugh; he helped bridge the culture

chasms; he made fun of Germans, and he made fun of my attempts at the German language and Americans in general. He had visited the United States several times and loved it there, but he said that America had "too many fett (fat) peoples."

Hans asked me one Easter if I believed that Jesus rose from the dead. I said yes and then asked him the same question. After a pause he answered, "Viel-leicht [perhaps]!" He regularly went to mass where one of the priests was a friend. However, Hans wouldn't receive the sacraments from the friend. His reason: "I know too much about him. I get in the line of the other priest, but I make sure that my friend sees me!"

Several years after moving back to the United States, Ruth and I traveled with our church choir on a trip into what had been East Germany. There was a final concert in Munich after we left eastern Germany. Hans and other German friends had come down from northern Germany to visit with us. After the concert, we were bidding one another good-bye, when an officer of the church where the choir had sung came up and gave me a sizable amount of money received as an offering for the choir from the people who had been present.

I said, "No, no, no! Give that money to Brot für die Welt" [Bread for the World, an organization that fights world hunger]. I handed the money to the lady who had given it to me. Hans was there, and he took the money out of her hands and handed it back to me. Mocking me, he said, "Nein, nein, nein! Bier für de Chor [beer for the choir]!"

Hans is like the others who refuse to let me be something I am not. All members of the clergy should have such a group of friends who love them, accept them as they are, but who are not particularly impressed with their divinity.

# Buck and the Band of Angels

I T WAS THE EARLY 1970S, AND A WORLDWIDE
social phenomenon was underway. Colonies of
European nations had declared themselves free and independent nations; there was an unpopular war in Southeast
Asia that was being protested; there was a general political
unease worldwide. There were revolutionary young people
in the West who did their own version of the Maoist Cultural
Revolution that began in China in the 1960s. There were
riots in the streets of Paris, political kidnapping and murder
in Germany, and the takeover by students of university
administration buildings in the United States.

Among those declaring themselves free and independent
were a large number of children and young teens. Many of
them were running away from home and living on the
streets. Some of them were experimenting with drugs and
sex. All of them were in danger.

The congregation I served was located near a city park
where many of those runaways from our city and surrounding towns hung out during the day and slept at night.
Responding to an invitation from a social agency that asked
our congregation to create a safe place for runaways

("undisciplined children," as the law designated them), we agreed. It was a huge success from the first night it opened and for the next twenty years. We called it The Relatives.

I was so busy looking for sustainable funding for The Relatives, I had little time to consider how we would staff the place. And then there appeared "Buck"—bright, amusing, and charming. He had a thousand-watt smile, long blond curly hair that hung down to his shoulders like one of *Charlie's Angels* (a popular TV detective show of the time), and he was barefoot. He had previously worked as a counselor in the juvenile court system. He knew what he wanted done and had a plan to get there. He hired seven more counselors like himself. I alternated between calling them "a bunch of leftover "flower children" and "a band of angels." They were both. I experienced them as keen-witted and astute—nervy, savvy, wise. Their style was different from mine, but I loved them because they loved our clients, they loved their work, and they were effective.

They were sweet people with the right convictions. They were also tough people who were realists about the task we had chosen. They understood these kids, and whereas I operated out of romantic notions of getting families back together, they knew that some families didn't want to make the attitude adjustments that were required to effect reconciliation. Some kids were not wanted back home. These counselors also understood the darkness that lived in and motivated some of our young clients. Youths up to eighteen years old were allowed to stay at The Relatives. Some months after The Relatives opened, the local morning newspaper headlined a murder that had taken place in a convenience store near the university. A female employee in the all-night store had been gunned down by a seventeen-year-old boy.

I was at The Relatives that morning after, and one of the counselors was reading the newspaper article. He looked up and said: "I think we had that kid here for a couple of nights recently."

He went to the card file where all the clients were listed and immediately retrieved his card. He read the comments written by another counselor who had dealt with the boy while he was there. It said, in big block letters, "THIS KID IS CRAZY AS S***."

I told you that our counselors were nontraditional people. I also said that they were perceptive.

I spent most of my time raising money. I went before the County Commissioners so many times they called me by my first name; likewise the City Council. Each thought the other should fund our work.

I spoke to church groups, service clubs, and book clubs. The general population was supportive and generous, with the exception of a few contentious grumps who challenged us by saying that such a facility would encourage children and young people to run away.

In a short time, there were so many invitations to speak to groups that I encouraged the inviters to ask one of our counselors. One inviter responded by saying: "Mr. Montfort, the membership of our club is rather conservative. I've seen some of your counselors and I think it would be best if you came." I went and they gave me five hundred dollars.

Buck and I decided that we should approach a well-known man in town and request a grant from his family's endowment trust fund. The appointment was made and as we parted the afternoon before, I said to Buck, "I want you to wear shoes and a shirt with a collar and sleeves." He laughed and promised not to embarrass me.

As I drove away, I realized that there was nothing about Buck that embarrassed me; he was real. I was the phony. Sometimes I was so conformable to my culture that I allowed the prejudices of others to shape me.

The next day, I drove to The Relatives to pick up Buck, and he came out wearing shoes (actually, sandals) and a shirt with a collar and long sleeves. He had washed his hair and taken it out of his usual ponytail, and his golden locks did indeed made him look like Farrah Fawcett-Majors, the actress from *Charlie's Angels*, but not much.

We drove to the man's office. I parked, and I tried hard not to say it, but the words just popped out: "Buck, I think you should button up your shirt." It was a kind of silky thing unbuttoned almost to his waist.

He flashed one of his fabulous grins and asked, "You think so? I think he might like this."

I laughed, but I insisted he button up. He did.

We didn't get any money.

# Bewildered Soul

**H**IS LETTER WAS ON MY DESK THAT MORNING, hand-delivered sometime the day before. It was signed "Bewildered Soul," along with his name. He had been in and out of the church several times of late—always with requests for money, something to eat, a jacket. He was bright and articulate, but he drank too much and he couldn't seem to get his intelligence and verbal abilities to work for him. The letter was an account of one of his more recent acts of beggary.

"Bewildered Soul" was only one of a succession of such folk I saw who stumbled from drink to drink; from handout to handout; from church to church; unkempt and heavy with the rancid odor of sweat, urine, smoke, and cheap wine. There were more than a few who came regularly to our church and some whose chutzpah was deftly played out with histrionic art.

Billy Hoover was another of our "regulars" and, I might add, he was also one of the best. He was really good at what he did. One of his finest performances began when my colleague and I exited the church building one day and ran up on him sitting against the wall of a protected entranceway, too intoxicated to stand. He had already been to the church several times in the week previous, and we had given him something each time.

He flagged us down. We stopped to speak.

Billy was irritable and contentious. He demanded that we give him some money. I said that we were on our way to an appointment and I wasn't going to give anything to him while he was in such a crabby mood.

He propped himself up on his elbow, used his other hand to point to the two of us, and pronounced, "There they are—two high-up muckedy-mucks." Turning his finger back toward himself, he said, "And here is poor little Billy Hoover." And with hardly a breath in between, he declared, "I'm going to report you to the United Way!"

On another occasion, Billy approached me while I was helping set up the social hall for a dinner that evening. Billy came in and followed me about, asking for some money. I told him I was busy and couldn't help him just then, to which he responded that my predecessor, Tom, had always given him what he asked for.

I set down the table I was carrying, turned toward Billy, and responded by pointing while saying, "He's not here anymore; he lives in Asheville, North Carolina, and it's that way." Billy departed in high dudgeon. (Ordinary people don't do high dudgeon anymore; Billy had perfected it to an art form.)

He went next door to the parsonage where my colleague lived, rang the bell, and when my colleague's wife answered, Billy asked to speak with the pastor. She inquired, "Which pastor?" To which he replied, "The good one, not that little fat one; if he's a pastor, then I am the President of the United States!"

Not many such people live their sad lives with such flair. But Billy wasn't the only one accomplished in the art of mooching. Bewildered Soul was good at it too. In the body of his letter, he reported that a couple of weeks before, he had gone to a restaurant at the Hyatt Regency Hotel, no money in his pocket, ran up a bill for $144.45, and was consequently arrested for "defrauding an innkeeper." He wondered if I could help him.

Bewildered Soul, Billy, and the others are easy to dislike. They are habitually lost—mock people. They look like people and at times talk like people, however confused and dishonest the talk may be; but there is no will there except toward the next drink, and the chief goal is survival—or maybe it is death. That kind of person is easily despised when you yourself are soaped and deodorized.

In one parish, we had a standing relationship with a nearby restaurant to feed that kind of person until one day the lady there called me and told me to never send another one there because if they had money to drink, they had money for food. Which was a very good argument. Except the ones I sent there had lost the ability to make that decision long before I saw them. I thanked her for her help in the past; I thanked her for bearing that burden for me.

I have always had an uneasy conscience when I deal with such people as Bewildered Soul and Billy. What does help look like to them? What is my responsibility? To the beggar? To the innkeeper? To the restaurateur? To the rest of society?

I find that I have to set aside all my usual criteria in order to deal with this one person whose needs are much bigger than the next meal or even the next drink. I find myself wondering, "Can this really be a human being?" Well, as much a human being as the man who wonders.

We are all of us lost, more or less, only my waywardness may not be as apparent as his. So I give him a meal or perhaps another drink and in so doing acknowledge how we are in this together.

Good luck, Bewildered Soul, and peace! Wherever you are now.

# FFV

ONCE HEARD HER IDENTIFY HERSELF AS AN FFV—a descendant of one of the First Families of Virginia. She often rhapsodized her beginnings in western Virginia and spoke of "Cousin Richard" and what he had to say about this or that. "Cousin Richard," who also was native to western Virginia, was known to the rest of us as Richard J. Reynolds, founder of the Reynolds Tobacco Company.

She periodically stopped by the church to instruct me on ways to more effectively do my work as pastor.

As my office faced the driveway leading up to the main entrance of our building, I could see who was coming and going. If I was alert, that vantage point allowed me time to gather my gumption before having to face someone who might not wish me well.

One morning I heard a car door slam and I looked up to see Effie. (That wasn't her real name; it's just a riff on FFV.) She was entering the church at a very purposeful pace. I quickly rose from my chair and closed the door between my office and that of my secretary and then settled back at my desk.

I could hear her asking the secretary if I was in. Then, without any announcement, she burst through the door, and as if it were part of the same action she began in a strident voice: "Tell me that what I've heard is not true!"

Without even getting up, I turned my chair toward her and said: "Effie, you are first going to have to tell me what it is you have heard." To be honest, I was dissembling and stalling; I was pretty sure that I knew what she had heard, but I wasn't going to help her say it.

"Tell me", she demanded, "that we are not going to have a Negro as our district superintendent!" (In our denomination, a district superintendent oversees the work of forty to sixty pastors and the parishes they serve).

"Effie," I replied, "I can't tell you that, because I think that we very well could have a black pastor as our district superintendent. I have heard that such an appointment has been projected."

And then, with a great sweeping motion, pointing somewhat indistinctly at something pictured in her mind, she said: "When that happens, you can move my membership to the Moravian Church."

"That is a decision that you will have to make," I replied, "if such an appointment happens."

"I've already decided. The day that happens, you can move my church membership to the Moravian Church."

She gathered her furs around her shoulders and exited as dramatically as she had arrived. It was all over in about sixty seconds.

Within a few weeks, the announcement was made that our new district superintendent was an African American man; his would be the first such appointment made in the southeastern United States.

No more than a few days after the announcement, I was in a meeting of clergy representing a number of Christian denominations. Bill, pastor of a nearby Moravian congregation, asked me about the announcement, and we and several other pastors discussed the ramifications.

After the others had dispersed, I said to Bill: "There's something you need to know. Effie has told me that she is going to join your congregation when that happens."

He knew Effie; she was an acquaintance of his mother. He raised his eyebrows and quietly said, "She shouldn't do that. She needs to know that the president-elect of the Moravian Church is a black man..." After a pause, he went on "... married to a white woman."

# Church Bullies

I LEARNED MUCH FROM THE PEOPLE IN MY first parish, who were farmers and industrial workers. I had heard their language long enough and listened to their stories carefully enough to recognize that there were huge themes coursing through the way they reported their lives. They required understanding; they were suspicious of people in authority, and they exercised a kind of aggressive anxiety that grew out of their fear that they would not be taken seriously. The result was that a few bullies, led by a man called Uncle Martin, had taken control of congregational life, terrorizing others and reigning with bluff and bluster.

The bullies turned on me as well, when on occasion my own understanding of how the work of the church was to be accomplished collided with their devious despotism. At such times, I often found myself standing alone. Others in the church had learned long before I arrived that they didn't want to rile the wrath of their particular oligarch. They were not sure that the autocratic voice of Uncle Martin should be silenced; they had depended so long on his bad disposition to get things done.

A man named Grover decided early on that I was somebody he didn't like, and he set out to intimidate me. He cornered me one night after worship and informed me that the church had allowed the Matthew Zink family to bury their father in one of his burial plots. He said he was going to sue the church. I said that I didn't think the lots were his; the cemetery belonged to the entire church. And while he had in his mind that there were eight plots that belonged to him, he had no deed to those plots, not even a letter confirming his claim. When I said that, he amended his earlier statement and declared in a loud voice, "I am going to sue the church and I am going to sue *you*!"

Some other folk standing around heard that and watched as he got into his automobile and scratched off in a cloud of dust down the unpaved road that passed the church. Mose, who had heard the last thing Grover said, came over to where I was and said, "Russ, he doesn't even belong to the church."

Grover never brought up the cemetery plot again, but he found other ways to harass me. That congregation had never used worship bulletins before my arrival, but I cranked them out without so much as a "by your leave, may I do this?" After that fateful night in the cemetery, Grover, who always sat about halfway back on the center aisle, would wait until he was sure I was looking, and then he would roll up his bulletin in a little ball and toss it like a basketball out into the aisle. Where it would take a couple of bounces and stay throughout the sermon as a tacit expression of the disrespect with which he held me.

I had to admit that it was an elegantly conceived insult. Grover was not to be trifled with. I would say that he was in about the ninety-fifth percentile of "disrespecters" in Randolph County.

Grovers are frequently found among us. Their dial seems to be permanently set on "aggressive." We find ourselves avoiding them, or avoiding the places where they hang out. Charlie Brown's friend Lucy is a bully. She is in charge of everything. You do it Lucy's way or you go home.

In conversations here and there, I hear people drawing a distinction between "aggressive" and "assertive" behavior, with the latter being more concerned with one's claim on one's rights, or those things which one perceives as one's entitlements or prerogatives. The Grovers of this world just take, by force or intimidation.

It's a tough world out there. The rules keep changing, and the details are getting so complex that the temptation is to decide issues according to whose mind is the cleverest or who has the biggest muscles or who has the biggest mouth.

All the more reason, I think, that truly adult people (in the church or out of the church) need carefully to assess their ways of negotiating with one another—to be certain that they don't deal with others in daunting ways. I decided somewhere back there that it is possible to stand up straight, assert my position, and hold my ground without acting scary or tyrannizing others. But not without first suffering some disquieting angst.

That decision has meant, however, that I have to hang my identity on some peg outside myself. If I have to rely solely on what I know of myself, from inside myself, I get timid and find myself doing one of two things—surrendering to the bully or raising my voice in a little terrorizing of my own.

But if I am empowered by the Spirit of Christ, then I find resources to lead me through what needs to be done, as well as grace enough to get me through the times I fail. Not even swaggering, swashing church bullies can intimidate me then. So there!

# Jesus Is There

RUTH WAS READING THE CHURCH NEWS-letter, which had just arrived in the mail. She said, "They are planning to start a Sunday school class of developmentally disabled adults at the church, and they are looking for volunteers. I think I will do that. Would you like to help?"

Without looking up from my newspaper, I said, "Yes, I like those people." I hadn't really thought that through, but the die was cast.

On Sundays for forty-three years, I had rolled out of my bed at 5:00 a.m. in order to get myself awake in time to arrive at the church with my mind in gear. Now that I was retired, for the first time in my life I had a pot of coffee and the Sunday *New York Times* and a long morning in which to delight. Once, I read that Michael J. Fox said that in his next life, he hoped to be reincarnated as a Jew so that on Sunday mornings he could go to the deli. I found that appealing.

I had arranged my Sunday schedule in such a way that I could skip Sunday school and arrive at the church just as the choir was processing down the aisle and the 11:00 a.m. service was getting underway. Also, there was usually a parking place up close to the church building vacated by some person who had attended an earlier service or had been at Sunday school.

I would scoot down the side aisle while all the other worshipers were "canticling God's glory." Along about the third stanza, when the sopranos went into their descant, I would slip into an available pew near the front and spiritedly sing the last verse. When the others closed their hymnals and looked up, there I was, looking enthusiastically engaged.

The new plan involving the developmentally disabled people meant that I was back in Sunday school. Which I hadn't meant to be. On the second or third Sunday of our new endeavor, I was sitting in worship among six young men with disabilities, partly listening to the sermon and partly sorrowing over my return to captivity. I don't remember the context of the sermon, but the preacher recounted the story of Mother Teresa and how, when asked how she could go into the streets of Calcutta and pick up all those dying men, she had answered, "Each one is Jesus in a distressing disguise."

I took a mental *luftpause* and said to the preacher (not aloud, of course): "George, that is so 1970s. Everybody in this church has heard that story *ad nauseam*." The way I knew it was that I had used the story *ad nauseam* in my own sermons.

I shifted my position in the pew, looked up, and there they were: six Jesuses sitting quietly among the worshipers, depending on me to tell them what would happen next and to see that they got back to their van.

Things generally proceeded well as we all learned to know one another. One of the men told me one day that he was going to look for a new class. He wanted to attend a "Christian" class. I was puzzled, since each Sunday we used the preacher's text for that day as a preparation for worship, and I asked for a clarification. He said that our class was boring. I said, "Tell me some things you would like to talk about in our class. We have been reading the Bible and talking about that. Tell me some topics you would like to discuss." Without a pause he responded, "How about electronics?"

Over a period of several years the class has grown, and the cadre of leaders has multiplied. A small community has grown up around these special people. It is church. Mostly what is happening is that we are all drawn into a simpler, sweeter, less complex community than "church" is—usually.

We talk about everything. Anything. And sometimes we are not all talking about the same thing at the same time. And the wondrous thing is that it doesn't matter.

Recently, thinking that the upcoming sermon on the trans-figuration of Jesus might be difficult for the group to understand, Ruth and I decided that we would talk about Lent, which began on Wednesday of that week. I asked, "What do we call this coming Wednesday?" "Ash Wednesday," came back the reply. They remembered. And I outlined the sequence of events of the next forty days, and came upon Good Friday. Hoping to draw them into the story, I asked, "What happens on that Friday before Easter?" Silence.

I gave some clues, but only Bennie had a response. He didn't talk clearly, and I had a hearing disability, so I didn't understand. As we often did, we asked him to go to the chalkboard and write out what he had to say. We watched with anticipation, and he wrote out in large capital letters *B B Q*.

There will be a barbecue on the Friday before Easter.

Actually, the information we share is the least of what we pass around in our group. Love is there, and acceptance. There is a sizable margin for error. There is a sweet spirit there, even though at times we have to help residents of group homes negotiate their interpersonal relationships.

We call ourselves the Joy Class, and there is merriment when we sing, "Jesus is a Rock, and he rolls my blues away," to the point that some class members get up and dance.

Not all class members get there all the time, of course, but Jesus is always there.

# Leandra

I T'S NOT AS IF RETIREMENT SNEAKS UP ON you, and suddenly one day there you are without a job. You turn over and discover that the alarm clock didn't go off because you didn't set it because this is the first day of the rest of your life. Someone else is doing the job that once was yours; you have to decide whether you are going to sign up for some other work or just hang out.

I thought about going for one of those jobs at the airport, driving the cart up and down the concourse calling out, "Watch out for the cart," and never stopping; or perhaps one of those jobs at the Department of Motor Vehicles where you get your license renewed and they never look at you; or one of those telephone jobs explaining the Medicare drug benefit for seniors. Of course, that would mean I would have to understand the Medicare drug benefit for seniors.

In my recent retirement years, I have worked as a custody advocate for an agency that tries to resolve child custody disputes. I've been at the Children's Law Center for about eight years, and I have discovered that there is no typical case. I am consistently "struck all of a heap" (as a man in my first parish used to say) at the myriad ways adults can devise to abuse, heckle, and harass their own children. Sometimes little children. What they intend is to provoke and peeve the other parent of their child, but in the process they also often pick off the child, like those guys up in D.C. who shot people at gas pumps, at the mailbox, or at the bus stop and sometimes missed their target and hit someone else.

One day last week I sat in a courtroom and listened to the testimony of a mother from whom custody of a little girl had been taken. The mother sat there—pretty, poised, teary, and under oath. She was responding to the examination of one of the attorneys; she was so aggrieved at the situation in which she found herself, it was difficult for her to talk. The father had taken the little girl out of school and to his home when he discovered that her mother was in the hospital. The most stunning part of what was happening was that the mother was decorating her story with breathtaking lies. I guess in psychological terms, one could describe her behavior as schizoid. She was creating her own reality as she talked.

The child whose custody was being contested by her mother and father was named Leandra. She was eight years old. Her mother had a history of drug abuse; her father had been arrested more than once for assault. Leandra was small for her age and wiry. She had a stolid expression and wore her hair in tight little braids that fell down and framed her sad little face.

The first time I saw Leandra, I watched her at play with a therapist. They were competing in a game in which she had to make decisions about the placement of discs that would cut off the progress of her opponent. It was like an enlarged 3D version of tic-tac-toe. When the therapist made a move, Leandra would sit there for a few moments, looking intently at the entire arrangement, and then she would decisively make her move, effectively blocking her opponent. Time after time.

After the game, Leandra and I talked some about her life. I asked her about her grade in school. She responded that she was in the second grade and immediately volunteered that she had failed the first grade because she couldn't read.

When I asked her about her life at home, she told me that she used to live with her mother but now she lives with her father. She said that she didn't like her mother because her mother called her stupid and would sometimes hit her on the head. And that her mother once told her to steal a toy from a store, which she did, but she "knew it was wrong," and later, when her mother asked her to do it again, she refused.

Leandra also told me that once her mother asked her to pee in a little bottle, and she did. I asked why her mother wanted her to do that, and as Leandra did with any question she didn't want to answer, she shrugged her shoulders. But it was she who had brought the topic up; it was she who looked me straight in the eye and shrugged, as if to ask, "Just how dumb are you?"

At the hearing, the judge gave temporary custody to the father and said the mother could have a supervised visit of two hours each Tuesday from 3:00 p.m. to 5:00 p.m. in the office of a social worker at the Department of Social Services.

Observing the visits through a one-way window is like a trip to the circus to watch the high-wire aerialists. It puts a knot in your stomach as you wait to see what disastrous thing might happen next.

The mother always arrives in the company of six or seven other people, most of them children who she identifies to Leandra as "your cousins." Also in the group is the mother's boyfriend, referred to as "your uncle." After one visit, when I asked Leandra who was with her mother, she was unable to identify any of the group but one cousin and the "uncle." During the last visit I observed, the role of boyfriend was played by someone else, who was introduced to Leandra as "your new uncle."

I was startled to observe the mother's behavior during these visits. Upon arrival for the first visit, she moved to turn on the television set in the room. When the attending social worker objected, the mother inquired if there was a radio. Again the social worker said no.

The "cousins" spread out in the room, making a lot of noise as they played with available toys. The oldest of the "cousins" situated herself between the social worker and the mother, who was talking softly with Leandra. So many dopey things were being said that you wondered if she could be serious.

The mother seemed to have no ability to evaluate her own behavior. I wondered how she could be so clueless. She questioned the circumstances of Leandra's life in her father's house. She was particularly interested in what the father's wife said and did. The mother told Leandra that she didn't have to do what the stepmother told her to do.

Leandra's father is a shy, handsome man with an engaging smile, but he makes only a thousand dollars a month and is married to a woman who is just twenty years old and in her fifth pregnancy. Some of these pregnancies were terminated. When the nextbaby arrives, there will be the parents and three children in the home.

One day in the not-distant future, I will be summoned to tell the court what I think is the best option for Leandra— where she will be safest; where she will be most respected; where, by some twist of fortune, she might be loved.

I am most impressed with how Leandra has not given into her mother's grotesque goofiness. Her mother ridicules her: "You have big feet; I have small feet. You got those big feet from your father." Relative to a Mother's Day card Leandra had made for her: "You made me a card? Your daddy didn't give you money to get me a real card? He's crazy. Why didn't he give you five dollars to get a card for me?"

In a discussion about the baby that her father's wife was expecting, Leandra's mother said, "Maybe that baby will be an albino; you know your daddy has an albino trait in him." Then this: "Your daddy is not buying you name-brand shoes anymore? I always bought you name brand. Now that your daddy has a new wife and baby, he can't buy name brands anymore."

During the course of this diatribe, Leandra never said a word; she never protested. When her mother criticized her appearance and remonstrated with her for something she had or hadn't done, Leandra never objected, never whined, never explained. She was quietly self-possessed.

During all that time, I was sitting in a small, darkened room adjacent to the play room watching what was happening through a one-way window. Once, someone else came into the room where I was sitting and turned on a light. That meant that I was visible in the room where Leandra was. She turned and looked, and her eyes settled on me; neither of us acknowledged the other. The light in my room was flicked off. She could no longer see me.

Not immediately, but some ten or fifteen minutes later,

Leandra asked the social worker, "Where did that guy go?" When the social worker asked, "What guy?" Leandra answered, "The one who comes here and talks to me."

"He is in another part of the building," the social worker answered. Leandra's mother wanted to know what man they were discussing, and the social worker told the mother that she had met me in a previous meeting, and the mother remembered and the topic was dropped. Leandra didn't tell them that she had seen me through the window.

There will be no best outcome here, but I find myself relying on Leandra. She is very wise. If I can hear enough of her story, if I can learn to listen to her, she will find a way—she will help me find a way.

# Showtime

PRESIDING OVER MARRIAGES WAS A BIG PART of my work as a pastor. It was often one of the more trying aspects of my profession. Many times there was a culture clash between how the church viewed the marriage ceremony and how the culture wanted to celebrate it.

The church has for some centuries now embraced the institution of marriage and has even developed an authorized ritual by which the event is shaped. It didn't always. Marriage was originally more like a business agreement. It had to do with the acquisition of property and the establishment of the right to inheritance. It was later that the church took it in and sanctified it, even calling it one of the seven sacraments.

Our denomination came out of the Church of England in 1784 and brought with it the rituals penned by Thomas Cranmer more than two hundred years before that. Until fairly recently, there was still in that service a moment when the man placed a wedding band on the woman's left hand and said, "With this ring I thee wed, and with all my worldly goods, I thee endow."

That reminds me of how we had to struggle with "thees"

and "thous" and other old-fangled phrasing such as "and thereto I plight thee my troth." Ruth and I plighted our troth as late as 1954.

Well into the twentieth century, a wife was asked in the ceremony, "Wilt thou obey him (and) serve him?" but he didn't promise to obey her or serve her. He wasn't asked to do that, but he had said that business about endowing her with all his worldly goods. I guess it was considered a trade-off. She would obey him, and he would give her his stuff.

Fortunately, the church rethought and rewrote the service about twenty years ago and dropped that anachronous language and came up with a strong service of mutual commitment that is more expressive of our current understanding of gender roles.

It wasn't the ritual that made my participation in weddings difficult, however; it was all the other stuff that got itself attached to the celebration. Engagement parties and rehearsal dinners with their own rituals and wedding directors (some from department stores and some from the florist and some from companies set up "to serve the wedding industry," none of whom could be classified as disinterested persons)—all complicated the wedding.

And sometimes there were small children in the service. Once there was a ring-bearing little boy who pooted all the way through the service in what I vow sounded like a *bossa nova* rhythm. I had a difficult time keeping the best man focused and on task.

One couple was determined to have communion at their otherwise uncomplicated wedding. It was just the two of them and a witness that I had rounded up on the way to the chapel. I went by the sacristy and looked in the refrigerator and lo, there was a chalice already filled with juice and a paten on top. I grabbed it and carried it along with me. I did the ritual up until the time to serve the elements. I took the paten off, and there were big green globs of mold floating around in the juice.

I had a napkin in my hand, and I pushed the mold to one side and held the glob with the napkin and held the cup high so that the couple would not see it. They were almost on tip-toe when they finally got a sip. They couldn't see the mold, but there was a new risk of getting juice up their noses. The bride did get a little bit on the end of her nose. I reached over with my napkin and wiped it off, which surprised even me.

Speaking of weddings and communion, there was a marriage that took place on the Cedar Island-Ocrakoke Ferry down on the North Carolina coast, during which the maid of honor carried "a handmade basket of bread for a communion between the bride, groom, and seagulls."

And then there was Libby, who joined our church somewhat anonymously and then turned up on the church

wedding calendar about six months out. She and her intended did their marriage preparation in an all-day Saturday
retreat setting with other couples from our congregation, and
though I had no previous acquaintance of them, somehow I
was written into the strategic plan as the celebrant.

On the night of the rehearsal, I asked the couple for the
license. I had previously had my assistant call and ask for it.
I didn't get it. On the night of the wedding, I still did not
have it. I couldn't locate the groom, so I went to the bridal
parlor and asked Libby for it. She informed me that they had
already married, four months previously.

I asked, "And what are we doing tonight? What's this
about?" She replied, "You know, every girl wants a big
church wedding." And I responded, "No, I didn't know that."
I went on: "Now, I want you to understand the process here.
You bring a license to me, issued by the county, and I am
authorized by the state to conduct this marriage. You don't
give me such a license; I have no authorization; there will be
no wedding."

"Mr. Montfort, you know you wouldn't do that!"

"Actually," I said, "I am just about to do it. I'm going to
find your groom."

On the way there I looked for Ruth, who was working the
wedding as a member of the wedding committee. I figured she
would be a calming influence and so I asked her to come along.

I turned the interrogation of the groom over to her, and she was talking to him in her indoor elementary teacher voice while I was trying to dope out what I would do. It was now 7:40 p.m.; the wedding was scheduled for 8:00.

I heard the groom say that he had the paper confirming their marriage, delivered to him by the civil officer who had married them. It was in his glove compartment. I said, "Go get it." At least it would tell me that they had procured a license.

By 8:00, I had decided that I would go on with the service, and along the way I discovered that everybody in the place but me knew the circumstances.

The groom was from a prominent Roman Catholic family in our town and his father was his best man. I made my decision and walked briskly to the door where the groom and his father waited. I was to enter by that door also.

The organist struck up the Jeremiah Clarke "Trumpet Tune," and that was our cue. Before I could open the door, the father sort of screwed up his face and stood very tall and crowded in close to me. "I hear that you're bothered about doing this wedding," he said.

"Y-e-a-h," I said. "I am bothered, and I would think you would be more bothered than I. In your faith tradition, marriage is a sacrament. Maybe you can tell me what kind of arrangements you made in your head that allow you to participate in a fake sacrament—something that would encourage me to go out there and fake a sacrament."

The "Trumpet Tune" was growing more insistent. I pushed the door open and said, "Showtime!" Then I walked through.

# Solemnizing the Rites

IT HAS BEEN SOME TIME NOW SINCE I HAVE SEEN a wedding announcement that spoke of the rites of marriage as having been solemnized. More often these days they are "celebrated." There was one marriage reported in our local paper during which the bride and groom, their friends and family, and the "celebrant" all gathered just inside the entrance of Kmart. They waited there for the blue light special to be announced, and while the light was flashing and the siren sounding, they all ran to the blue light location. Not to buy anything of course, but to get married there. Who knew that was an option?

Those rites were not solemnized. No way. But it sounds like fun.

My friend told me that his daughter was married a couple of weeks ago, and it was a splendid celebration. He had never seen her more radiant; nor had he participated in a marriage service more meaningful. He thinks the "celebrant" was someone they procured online. I didn't ask.

I have noticed in some wedding announcements issuing from California of late, occasionally a friend of the bride or groom has been authorized to solemnize the rites—just for that couple on that day. Maybe you can do that online. Get authorized, that is. Or even get married, for that matter. It is California, after all.

All of that leading up to this: Perhaps we have arrived at the era of the clergyless wedding. And I think a lot of people are going to be happier.

One of the turning points for me came at a formal Saturday evening wedding. The groom and his groomsmen were all military officers. They were an attractive, exuberant bunch. One of the men had been designated as the soloist for the wedding.

On the night of the rehearsal, the organist slipped into my office to tell me that the soloist couldn't locate the pitch, no matter how loudly the organist played it. I suggested that the organist ask the soloist to sing at the reception following the ceremony. The soloist (known henceforth in this recounting simply as S) didn't take kindly to the suggestion.

After the rehearsal, S announced that he was going to make a speech prior to singing his song. Through the organist, I sent a message that it would be inappropriate for him to make a speech.

On the wedding night, I was back in my office preparing for the ceremony when the organist slipped in again with the news that S intended to make his speech regardless of whether it was thought by some to be inappropriate.

I left my desk and went to a door that opened into the chancel area, where S had situated himself to sing. When he looked up, I motioned for him to come speak to me. He came.

I said to him that he was not to make a speech. He could save his speech for the reception. He informed me that he was going to do it during the ceremony, that the church was not mine. "It is God's church!" he declared.

"You're right," I said, "and there is a clear line of command here." I used a military metaphor, hoping he would resonate to that. "This is God's church, and God put me in charge of it. And our denomination gives me the authority to shut this wedding down, should I choose. You make that speech and we will all be embarrassed—including the bride, her family, and your friend, the groom." He didn't make the speech.

Fortunately, more people are deciding that they should not have their wedding in a church. As a result, they won't have to decorate the church like a bordello; they won't have to smuggle liquor into the bride's room; they can have photographers set up right in the bride's face; there will be nothing they can't do. There will be nothing to sneak by the preacher.

I recently saw a wedding announcement that told of a couple who married "at midnight on January 1 at the Little

White Wedding Chapel Drive-Thru Tunnel of Vows in Las Vegas, Nevada." They "drove through the tunnel on a Harley Red Horse and spoke their vows with a backdrop of fireworks welcoming the New Year." It said nothing about them "plighting their troth." I think they made the right decision.

And there was the couple up in Greensboro, North Carolina, who married at Emerald Pointe (a water amusement park), and after they were pronounced husband and wife, they went down the waterslide together. That sounds like a fun wedding, and it required no preacher and no wedding committee with guns strapped to their hips and a wedding policy in hand.

That wedding was outdone, I think, by the couple who got married at the start-finish line of the Southern 500 stock car race in Darlington, South Carolina. The wedding write-up, which appeared in the Lifestyles section of the paper, said "they got hitched without a hitch, and the large crowd was quiet and respectful during the ceremony, except for one racing fan who screamed, 'Don't do it! Don't do it!' "

Up in Clinchport, Virginia, a "bride and bridegroom exchanged vows in the bed of a 1999 Chevrolet 4x4 Silverado pickup truck decorated with white bows and mud. The bride wore camouflage hunting pants and a Dale Earnhardt shirt and cap. She carried a large bouquet of fresh flowers and fishing lures." The wedding party and guests spent the night camped on the banks of the Clinch River. I bet they had a good time. It was the right wedding for them.

There are some who almost get it right. Down in eastern North Carolina, there was a fairly traditional wedding in a church with many of the usual accoutrements: candlelight, lots of flowers, a predetermined color scheme including cummerbunds for the men in military camouflage, Alençon lace embroidered with pearls and sequins, a pianist, an organist, and a vocalist whose first name was Fuzzy. He sang "I Will if You Will." I read that in the paper.

My advice to people who want a memorable wedding different from the masses is to plan your own, wear what you like, serve what you want, and above all stay out of churches and do not invite a preacher to solemnize the rites (as they say). Preachers are assuredly opinionated and are no fun. You don't want an obnoxious ideologue at your party.

Personally, I don't do weddings. I don't even go; that's my gift to the couple.

# Funny Little Things

THE YEARS I SPENT IN GERMANY REQUIRED A focused mind, disciplined study, and a capacity for improvisation. There were a number of "funny little things" that unbalanced me—unexpected, unplanned incidents that required an agility of social response that I was not always able to rally.

When I told the people who interviewed me for the job that my proficiency in the German language was limited to counting from one to ten, they told me that I didn't need to know German. That was not true.

At age forty-nine, I set out to learn the language; Ruth and I took six hours of instruction every week in our home. While I never became fluent, I could negotiate my way through shopping, buying railroad tickets, crossing international borders, ordering coffee and cake in a Konditorei, and having my automobile serviced at the Audi dealership.

I always went at 7:00 a.m., just as the dealership's service department was opening, and I always waited for Herr Neuss to come out and assume his position at the counter. I knew it was his position because his name was posted there. I waited for him because he understood my German.

One morning, I arrived before any manager had assumed his post. There were about a half dozen of us customers standing about waiting. Soon, one of the service managers entered and took his position, and those waiting all went to him. Germans are not very good at queuing. I knew I wanted to speak only with Herr Neuss. I moved up to his position on the counter.

In a matter of moments, he came in and we exchanged greetings, and immediately some of the customers who had queued up in front of the other manager came back and petulantly complained to me that they had been there first.

I was in an expansive mood and decided that I would give up my place in line. As I stepped back, I invited them to get in front of me and they did. Three of them got in front of me.

While I was standing there feasting in my mind on the surpassing virtue of what I had just done, there entered an elderly gentleman, buttoned up in a cashmere overcoat with a silk scarf and kid gloves. He had all his auto repair papers in a small rectangular leather purse tucked under his arm. He lined up behind me and almost simultaneously dropped his purse, whereupon all his papers scattered, some up behind a potted palm tree. I stooped down and started retrieving them for him, even those behind the tree. As I straightened up and handed the papers to him, he took my place in line.

That was only one of a continuing series of cultural

entrapments to which I succumbed because I didn't really understand what was going on. The most shattering was yet to come.

Our congregation was exotic in its racial and linguistic mix. There were representatives of twenty-six countries, many from Asia and Africa. I found the interaction with them endlessly enthralling and I developed friendships among them.

One African lady, an officer of a West African embassy, was particularly charming, and we frequently had animated conversations. She was married to a Caucasian man, but it was not a congenial union. She asked me to come visit her in her home, where she wanted to discuss the matter with me.

I arrived mid-afternoon and was surprised to learn that she had prepared a full lunch for me. While I ate, she laid out for me her disappointment in her marriage. She was disappointed that she was childless but didn't think her husband, an undignified man whose behavior was often coarse, would be an appropriate parent. She might divorce and remarry. She would like to have a child with a refined and graceful Caucasian man.

I finished lunch and she went to get coffee. I wandered over to look at a huge, beautifully carved *schrank,* a freestanding closet similar to what we Americans now put the bedroom TV in and call it an armoire. *Armoire* is the French word for *schrank*. We had such a piece of furniture when I was growing up in rural Kentucky, only we called it a chifforobe, and my father hung his shirts in there and stashed his Knights Templar hat on the top shelf. The hat had an immense ostrich feather stretched along the top and looked like something out of a Gilbert and Sullivan operetta. I never saw him wear it. I couldn't even imagine him wearing it.

My hostess came back into the room with the coffee things on a tray, and I began a conversation with her about the schrank, asking how old it was and where they had found it. It was the kind of German thing cherished by foreign service workers from other parts of the world. Then they could take it back to their home country and say something like, "I picked that up at the flea market on the Poppeldorf Palace grounds."

I was concentrating on the carved detail when my hostess came up behind me and put her arms around my waist and leaned her head against my back.

I froze.

I thought, "Oh-my-gooodness!" It was more than an expletive. It was a sincere prayer. "Refined and graceful," I recalled she had said. How about "dumbfounded and fleet-footed"?

I don't remember the details of my departure, but it was immediate–and graceless.

# Premature Periods

**A**S MENTIONED PREVIOUSLY, EARLY IN MY career I worked for two summers at a newspaper, where among my responsibilities was writing a weekly advertisement disguised as a column. I didn't like the job, because I was required to write adulatory copy about some things of which I had no experience and some things that I knew but didn't like. How does one get lyrical over a set of dentures? ("Ready in only twenty-four hours!")

My most vivid memory of that department was that my immediate boss, whose name was Rory, hummed all day long, every day. He was also the one who signed off on the "Black as Sambo" fiasco. Rory hummed "Make Believe" all the time, a song from the musical *Showboat*. I arrived before he did on most days, and he would come through the door humming the tune. Usually I left before he did in the afternoon, and that same tune was the last thing I heard as I headed to the elevator.

"Make Believe" was a good theme song for what we did in that office. It was before the deceitful magic of digital cameras, where one can rearrange reality according to one's wishes. In a family portrait, one of my grandsons had his eyes closed, so the photographer took the open-eyed head from another photo of him and moved it to the desired photo.

At our office in the advertising department we had no digital cameras, of course; they hadn't been invented yet. But we were not without resource. It was in that office that I was introduced to the airbrush, which was a tool we used to make photographs look better than they did. We could remove crow's-feet and bags from under eyes and erase chins at the same time we took off weight and reduced the size of a model from size 14 to size 6.

With enough time and determination, we could refashion the world to fit our notion of how it ought to be. We could make the images fit the words. It was like being gods of our own universe.

It was a portent of things to come.

I discovered later in life that this particular state of things is characteristic of many worlds, not only the world of advertising. It is done with great skill by politicians. Preachers also are artful practitioners. In church. That is, they create universes of their own psychological and spiritual dimensions and ask people to live there, denying any truth that isn't understood there or anything that they can't reconcile with their preconceived judgments.

In Lewis Carroll's *Through the Looking Glass,* the White Queen and Alice engaged in a conversation about believing what one wants to believe regardless of the facts. Upon hearing the Queen claim that her age was "one hundred and one, five months and a day," Alice said, "I can't believe that!"

"Can't you?" the Queen said with a pitying tone. "Try again: draw a long breath, and shut your eyes."

Alice laughed. "There's no use trying," she said. "One can't believe impossible things."

"I daresay you haven't had much practice," said the Queen. "When I was your age, I always did it for half an hour a day. Why sometimes, I've believed as many as six impossible things before breakfast" [(Bloomsbury, NY, 2001) p. 92].

There are ideological preachers in ideological churches. You have to get past them on your way into the church. You have to pay homage to "eternal truths" that got that way by fiat or a majority vote and can easily become impossible things you have to sign off on if you mean to get into that church. Or stay there.

One American church teaches that every faithful male member of that church will have his own world (planet) to populate, which he goes to after death. There are lots of women there—his, so to speak. I don't remember how they get there. Women don't have much status in that church. (Martha Beck, *Leaving the Saints* [New York: Three Rivers Press, 2005], p. 82).

And in my town, there is a very capable woman who ran for office, but she first had to get the permission of the elders at her church. The elders are men.

There are assertions of faith that I gladly proclaim. I believe in God; I believe in Jesus Christ; I believe in the Holy Spirit. I believe in the Bible.

I also know myself to be alienated from God; I am a sinner.

For the rest, I try to hang loose and bring my deep faith in God, one of whose names is Love; my total commitment to Jesus, who revealed the God of Love to me; and the presence of the Holy Spirit to comfort and instruct me in those confounding circumstances that I will experience.

Jesus once said in response to a questioner's query: "Which commandment is the first of all?", The first is "Love the Lord your God with all your heart—soul, mind and strength and a second is like it "You shall love your neighbor as yourself." That's an effective synopsis of his teaching. Augustine said, "Love God, and do what you will." That's about as concise a statement on the ethical life as is possible, I think.

The church, on the other hand, has never been willing to let anything hang loose. There are always people who want to pass resolutions about this and that, and then see that they are published somewhere—published everywhere.

It is particularly alarming when it happens among religious people who turn opinions into dogma and start shutting down people who question them. The fearful part is when those people decide one day to settle for proximate truth and cut off debate and put down a period(.). A premature period(.). God, I think, is wary of the period(.). It might indicate closure and finitude that isn't there.

I like living in a world where the decisions are not yet all made because we don't have all the facts yet—that is, because God is still at work.

# God Is the Audience

THERE IS A LOT OF UNEXAMINED, BUMBLING silliness that goes on in the worship service at some churches. There was a church near our vacation house that we liked to attend. Nobody ever spoke to us, but the preacher was very good and she did the only viable "children's sermons" I have ever heard. She used the day's text. It worked two ways. Not only did she retell the lesson in such a way that it was accessible to children; it also got the older people there ready for the sermon coming up.

But they had a little ritual at the beginning of the service that I could never figure out. The choir processed down the center aisle, and as they reached the front of the chancel they would individually stop and make a little bow. There was no cross there, and they weren't bowing as they passed in front of the "host" (the consecrated bread of the communion, which in some Christian traditions is considered the real body of Christ, hence the genuflection every time they pass in front of it). It wasn't that.

There was no cross. There was a flower arrangement on the table, but nothing I could determine that should be addressed with the reverence of a bow. It seemed random to me. God knows that I don't think we treat God's great creation with enough respect, but an arrangement of flowers?

What happened as a result of the bows was that the singers processing, singing, and bowing had too many things to think about, and they would run into one another, like speeders on a foggy morning on the Interstate. I feared that somebody was going to get hurt. I never did figure that out.

The last time I preached was to help a young pastor who had just been appointed to a new parish. Since he couldn't get there for his first Sunday, he asked if I could help.

It was about an hour's drive, and Ruth and I made it in plenty of time to work out the logistics of the service. There were two churches on the circuit, and I was to conduct the worship for both congregations that morning. I had drawn up a fairly tight schedule, including the songs, lessons, prayers, hymns, and sermon.

The people there had other ideas. It was the Sunday preceding July Fourth, and during the first hymn a stalwart young man carried in the American flag and set it down right in front of the pulpit then they sang "The Star-Spangled Banner," pledged allegiance to the flag, and shared news about a number of illnesses in the community. They acknowledged the wedding anniversary of a couple, and one or two of the couple's children gave testimonies to the devotion shared by their parents.

There were four or five special musical numbers, and the service was handed over to me with only five minutes left before I was to strike out for congregation number two. In order to make eye contact with my listeners, I had to look around the flag, which was right up in my face. Five minutes was actually enough; I was glad to get out of there.

I heard a preacher on my car radio once who was getting very excited as his sermon unwound. Suddenly, he stopped and called out to someone there in the church, "Brother Sisk, come here and take this microphone; I've got to run a while." And Brother Sisk came and took over the sermon, and the radio listeners could hear the preacher running around the room, shouting. It got louder when he was approaching the front of the church and diminished as he ran toward the back.

And then there is the preacher who begins each sermon with a knock-knock joke. And there are the houses of worship that, no matter how small the room, have a battery of microphones and huge woofers and tweeters (low-frequency and high-frequency speakers)—more electronic equipment than a rock concert. And because the room is small, the sermon is heard better at the Pig and Whistle Café two blocks down than it is in the sanctuary.

Worship has become a sound-and-light show, with commercial production values, and worshipers have become "the audience." That's a twist. I've always thought of God as the audience.

# God Always Does

**S**O MUCH IS HAPPENING IN SO MANY PLACES that it is hard to stay focused. There are so many issues that demand my attention and my response—so many, in fact that the only way to handle the many is sometimes to ignore them all.

Discernment and discretion—both are needed. I must be able to choose from among my many options—choose in terms of what I might really expect to influence or effect.

Ruth has always been better at it than I. She's little and she doesn't look mean, but she's tough. Once, while working as a teacher of people with developmental disabilities, her principal told her one Friday that on Monday he was sending her another child. She reminded him that she already had the numerical limit that state law would permit.

He allowed as how he was the principal, she was getting another child come Monday. "Well," Ruth said, "he'd better be able to teach, because when he comes in, I go out."

On Monday, he came with another child.

On Monday, he also removed a child.

It really is not a case of who wins and who loses. It is a case of setting viable goals and knowing what is possible.

The trouble with many of us is that we are so overwhelmed by the larger task that we fail to see what we can do, and how to begin.

I pray each day that God will give me big visions and let me dream grand dreams. I pray also that God will show me how to make the first move; take the first step.

Not all the steps. Just the first one.

God does. God always does.